Covenant *of* Health

BEYOND A PROMISE

Dr. Beechard Moorefield

Eagles Nest Publishing

A Division of
Eagles Nest Forum, Inc.

Eagles Nest Publishing books may be ordered by contacting:

Eagles Nest Publishing
A Division of Eagles Nest Forum, Inc.
www.eaglesnestforum.com
moorefieldbeechard@gmail.com

1.336.399.4288

Scripture taken from the King James Version of the Bible.

ISBN: 978-1-7360289-1-9

Print information available on the last page.

Eagles Nest Publishing rev. date: 07/31/2021

ACKNOWLEDGMENTS

If you have ever succeeded at something that is truly worthwhile, you need to view that scenario as you would a turtle sitting on top of a fence post. When you get that image fixed in your mind, one conclusion can be automatically drawn that will be accurate without question. That conclusion is this – that turtle did not get there by itself.

While the writing of this book took place because I sat for many hours at my computer, making each key stroke that produced this document in its original form, there is a foundation of spiritual life, intellect, flesh, and blood beneath it that few will acknowledge, and that even fewer will ever have first-hand knowledge of who they are. To that foundation, I owe a major debt of gratitude.

My first acknowledgment requires me to look up and inward. Thank you, Jesus, for being my Lord, Savior, Healer, Provider, Deliverer, and Primary Encourager. I can do all things through Christ Which strengthens me, but only through Him.

Second only to God, and absolutely first in this life, I must look to my side; to my bride, my wife, my partner in life and ministry, prayer partner, mother of my sons, and my love, Sharon. She has filled all those roles with a divinely given grace, and she has done her work in excellence. I love her, am proud of her, and am eternally grateful to and for her.

Third, I must look down. And in the downward look, I must acknowledge that I look down on no one, but gratefully at so many. I refer to those on whose shoulders I have stood to reach higher, whose hands have given me a great boost to move forward, and whose life-filled eyes have helped me to see the unseen, and to never give up on a dream, especially when they believed God is in it. The numbers of shoulders on which I have stood, hands I have received, and well-illuminated insights I have received are too numerous to count, so their names will not be listed here. That would require a book unto itself. But to each of them, from the depths of my heart, I offer my sincerest and deepest thanks.

FOREWORD

When we hear the word salvation most people think only of giving their life to Jesus and going to heaven. However, a study of the original Greek word used for the term salvation reveals a much deeper and broader meaning. It includes, as Jesus said, life more abundantly. This new life includes not only healing, but divine health – living a life free from sickness and disease. This may be hard to believe, though it would appear that most are not living at this level of freedom, it doesn't diminish the truth of the Word of God.

In this book, Beechard Moorefield shows the reader from the Word of God strong, irrefutable truths that divine health is "*beyond a promise*" from God; it is a settled fact. It is challenging to read and wrap your head around such a truth, especially since the world is just beginning to return to normal from a pandemic. But God's Word is always true.

I ask you to read this book with an open mind. Try to block out prior teachings you may have heard, and even your own experience with sickness and disease. I, too, have had health challenges, and to be clear, I am not saying that these challenges will not come at us. However, when they do, rather than succumbing to the illness or even worse, agreeing to the sickness, fight knowing that you have been given a better life.

This teaching will give you the Biblical basis to build your faith to believe for that "better life." You can take charge of your life rather than just accepting that, "every year I get a cold or the flu." It doesn't have to be this way. We play an active role in this fight. We have to eat right and exercise. We can't abuse our bodies with alcohol and smoking. If we do the things that we should and stand on the Word of God, then our expectations should line up with the Word.

I pray that this book will open your eyes in a new way to your Covenant of Health from God, and you will begin to seek after this gift as you would for gold or a lost treasure. After all, divine health is one of the most valuable treasures one could ever find, and if you are a believer – it is "*beyond a promise*" to you. It is a **Covenant of Health**.

Jody Williams, MBA

AUTHOR'S INTENT

I have personally found 3 John 2 and 4 to be two of the most profound verses of Scripture I have ever applied to my own personal life. These two verses say, "Beloved, I wish above all things that thou mayest prosper and be in health, even as thy soul prospereth. I have no greater joy than to hear that my children walk in truth." (3 John 2 & 4)

These are two of the most powerful statements to be found as to what pleases our heavenly Father. While in their original writing, they were the words of John to those who loved and followed him, these are also the words of God to His Church. Our heavenly Father wants us healthy and prosperous, and for us to walk that way in this earth, we need to walk in the light of His Word. And that is His greatest joy and highest pleasure for each of His children.

And when we consider Hebrews 11:6, that "without faith it is impossible to please Him [God]," that places 3 John 2 and 4 in an even brighter light. The understanding to be gleaned here is that for us to walk and live in that highest desire God has for His children, we must do so by faith. 3 John 2 and 4 will not happen just because we happened to read it one day. We *must* apply our faith, and that diligently so, to living in that place in the Lord. It is there, in faith, that our Father will honor our work and life as pleasing to Him, and bring to pass in our lives the manifestation of His highest wish for His people.

My writing in the pages of this book is in no way intended to be mystical, foreign, or difficult to grasp. I have endeavored to use simple terms in a straightforward manner, my prayer being that anyone who reads it will straightway comprehend what Holy

Spirit is desiring to convey through me, and that I convey it accurately from His mind.

Allow me to further state that this writing, while in no way intended to be a textbook, may teach a great deal about healing and health for the believer. And while it is not, in any way, a reference book filled with quotes of great men, or modern-day experts in the arena of healing and health as it relates to the church, I believe you will find that great men who were writers of the Scriptures are indeed cited, quoted, and referenced.

The deepest intent of this writing is to offer to you, the reader, revelation knowledge on this sorely needed topic for the body of Christ. This writing has been lived, witnessed, demonstrated, and realized to be in harmony with God's Word. Read it, let it speak for itself, and as Holy Spirit leads you, apply it to yourself and your daily life.

I also believe that every word I write will ultimately have soul-prospering effect on you. That is, after all, the direct will of God, and will produce in your life His will made manifest before the world. To God be the glory for the marvelous witness that will make on every person your life touches.

To that end, I offer the following as a benediction over you and the time you invest in reading this book. It is from Ephesians 3:20 and 21. "Now unto Him that is able to do exceeding abundantly above all that we ask or think, according to the power that worketh in us, unto Him *be* glory in the church by Christ Jesus throughout all ages, world without end. Amen."

Covenant *of* Health

BEYOND A PROMISE

Contents

CHAPTER ONE

The Missing Element?

For years, Thomas Edison experimented with hundreds of different materials, attempting to determine what would make a proper filament for his incandescent light. He finally discovered what he needed, and when he introduced that element, he had invented the light bulb. For the believer, let me end much, if not all, of your experimentation. The element you are seeking is the Word of God, for it is the "entrance of the Word that brings light." (Psalm 119:130)

Joshua 1:8

*This book of the law shall not depart out of thy mouth;
but thou shalt meditate therein day and night,
that thou mayest observe to do according to all that is written
therein: for then thou shalt make thy way prosperous,
and then thou shalt have good success.*

Proverbs 4:20-22

*My son, attend to my words;
incline thine ear unto my sayings.
Let them not depart from thine eyes;
keep them in the midst of thine heart.
For they are life unto those that find them,
and health to all their flesh.*

Psalm 107:20

*He sent his word, and healed them,
and delivered them from their destructions.*

1 Peter 2:24

*Who his own self bare our sins in his own body on the tree,
that we, being dead to sins, should live unto righteousness:
by whose stripes ye were healed.*

This is a book about healing. More than that, it is a book about how to remain healed once the work has been accomplished. And this chapter deals with what I am convinced is the missing element in most lives where healing is needed.

That element is the Word of God. I am not referring to having one or two verses, or even one or two hundred verses on the subjects of healing and prosperity, committed to memory. I am speaking of having your spirit filled to overflowing with the riches of God's Word, having it hidden deeply within your heart, with your mind so influenced by it that your thinking is dominated by God's written Word.

Numerous are the Scriptures to which I could refer on this particular topic, but please allow me to deal with one passage in particular, that when taken in its context, tells the story clearly. That passage is John 8:31-32.

> Then said Jesus to those Jews which believed on him, If ye continue in my word, *then* are ye my disciples indeed;
>
> And ye shall know the truth, and the truth shall make you free.

Perhaps you have heard someone say the truth shall make you free. While those words are indeed taken from a statement by Jesus Himself, as a stand-alone statement, it is not true. Those six words are true only when taken in the context of the two verses cited. Look closely at what these two verses say.

First, Jesus spoke these words to people who believed on Him. The first thing a person should do is determine if he is indeed a believer. The remainder of these two verses, if to be fully applied to one's life, rests on the truth of whether one is a believer nor not.

Next, it should be noted that as a believer, you *must* continue in His Word. That means a lifelong commitment to the reading, study, and meditation of the Word of God, as well as obedience to the Word of God.

It is by these means, and in particular, the doing of the Word of God, that a person has the capacity to become a disciple of Christ. Simply put, a disciple of Christ is one who has disciplined himself to be a doer of the Word. The person who had done so is a true disciple of Christ.

It is then through this process of discipling one's self that one comes to a true knowledge of the truth of God's Word. When one does the Word, the Lord is faithful to carry out that Word toward the obedient disciple, as God "hasten[s] His Word to perform it" (Jeremiah 1:12).

Finally, it is by knowing the truth that one is truly made free. When one abides in the Word until he lives by it, and in so doing experiences the reality of the power of God to fulfill His Word, it is then that the greatest freedom one can know is manifest. A person who knows he can stand at all times on the truth of God's unchangeable Word, knowing that the Lord will be faithful to that Word, is absolutely free and unfettered by any chains that would prevent the full working of God in his life. You see, God has magnified His Word above all His Own Name (Psalm 138:2).

It is such a lifestyle that will bring a person to the point of living what could be called the life of *true soul prosperity*. Remember that term, for in this writing, you will surely see it again. I will deal more specifically with the nature of soul prosperity, how to have it, and how to see it work in your life to the glory of God. While in broad terms, the missing element in so many lives is the Word of God, it is more to the specific application of that Word that I will address the following chapters of this book.

Keep in your thinking as you read further, that you can have a prosperous spirit-man filled with the Word, and in your spirit, know the Word of God intimately. But please note that 3 John 2 declares the greater prosperity and health is determined by *soul prosperity*, not spirit prosperity. The less prosperous your soul is, the less likely you are to fully realize prosperity and health in your whole being. As incredible as it may seem, much of your future prosperity and health is dependent upon you and how you work in obedience to the Word of God to cause your own soul to prosper.

Please don't misunderstand me. You must feed your spirit man well on the manna of God's Word, and you must also look to the well-being and maintenance of the temple of Holy Ghost, which is your own body. It is not a matter of dealing with one or the other of your own triune being (spirit, soul, body). You are a spirit, you have a soul (mind, will, intellect, and emotions), and you live in a body. It is your own personal responsibility to feed your spirit man on the nourishing Word of the living God. It is also your own personal responsibility to tend well to your body, which is the temple of Holy Ghost. Don't fall short on either of these arenas.

But remember, too, it is so very important that you accept the responsibility to nourish and nurture your own soul, for it is as your soul prospers that you will ultimately prosper and be in health. And the greatest tool you have to achieve the soul prosperity you desperately need is the constant application of God's Word in your whole life, to your whole being, lending to its continual renewing of your mind.

CHAPTER TWO

A Second Opinion: A Better Opinion

Why do people price-shop? They're looking for a better deal. Why do people, especially with their doctor's recommendation, seek a second opinion? They're looking for a potentially better diagnosis, better outcome, and at the least, an accurate confirmation of what their doctor told them.

In the commodities market, why should one pay a certain price for something if the same product, or better, or equal service can be acquired for a lower price? The truth is, there is no good reason. Basic economics would indicate that fact.

By the same token, why should anyone, especially a Christian, accept the remedies offered by the world when a better, far better remedy exists? The answer there can sadly be seen in the ignorance that exists within the church. False teaching, failed teaching, faulty teaching, and flattering teaching seem to be the call of the age; church people who want to have their ears tickled with easy beliefism and little, if any, personal responsibility. It's time for men and women of God to set the record straight with accurate teaching of the Word that was sent to heal all who would hear.

Romans 3:4

God forbid: yea, let God be true,
but every man a liar; as it is written,
That thou mightest be justified in thy sayings,
and mightest overcome when thou art judged.

Hebrews 6:18

That by two immutable things,
in which it was impossible for God to lie,
we might have a strong consolation,
who have fled for refuge
to lay hold upon the hope set before us:

John 14:6

Jesus saith unto him,
I am the way, the truth, and the life:
no man cometh unto the Father, but by me.

In our extremely competitive world, I'm sure you often hear words like, "I'd get a second opinion." You hear it in relation to insurance estimates for auto repairs, or when someone doesn't like the opinion they receive from a lawyer, or even when a medical diagnosis leaves cause for possible doubt.

Perhaps you have been in a position in life where you would like to have second opinion. Maybe that house you wanted to buy was appraised too high for you to consider. Perhaps that car you wanted to trade was appraised too low for you to make the trade. Or is it possible that your doctor told you the disease that is attacking your body has no known cure, or even worse, says the disease is fatal and your life expectancy is, at best, short?

I can't help you with the house or the car, but I can surely help you with the healing/health question. What you need is a second opinion. And not just *any* second opinion. What you really need is a better opinion, and even better than that, the best opinion. And what's more, the second opinion of which I speak is really the *only* opinion you need. I have just the place for you to go. I know of a medical clinic that specializes in better opinions. I know a medical staff that refuses to accept anything less than better opinions. And I know a Chief of Staff Who has never lost a case. He knows there is no expiration date on you anywhere. His Name is Doctor Jesus.

He is the Great Physician. He is the Healer of Isaiah 53 and 1 Peter 2. He is the sight restorer of John 9. He is the Matthew 8 cure for fever. He is the leper cleanser of Mark 1, and the withered hand restorer of Mark 3 He is the Matthew 9 answer to palsy and the Luke 17 resolution to dropsy. The fact is that there is no sickness or disease, known or unknown, past, present, or future, that is outside the prognosis and cure offered by our Lord and Savior, Jesus Christ.

Since the beginning of history, mankind has been searching for a *panacea*, a magic cure-all for the ills of the world. There is no such thing as a magic cure-all for the world's ills. But when Jesus came, He did bring an answer, and not just any answer. He brought *The Answer*. He did not point to *a* way, or *several* ways, but declared Himself to be *The Way*. He did not refer to *a* truth, or *some* truth, but declared Himself to be *The Truth*. He did not speak of *a* life, or *some* life," but declared Himself to the *The Life*.

So, when I speak of a second opinion, or better opinion, I am not talking about some *pie-in-the-sky-by-and-by* dream. I am speaking of fact, settled truth, the ultimate solution.

Before I go forward from here, let me clear the air of possible misunderstandings. I am a Christian man, married with two sons and two grandsons. I have been, at this writing, engaged in ministry for 50 years, 28 of them as pastor of a wonderful congregation. I am a human being with human weaknesses, flaws, and frailties. Perfection is not one of my present human characteristics. Sickness and disease have attacked my body just like it has yours. I have a family doctor. He is a Christian and takes his profession and care of his patients very seriously. I have had the occasion to see him many times, and each time he has exhibited great professionalism, genuine concern, and gracious kindness as he examined, diagnosed, or treated me. His consummate approach made me comfortable that he is a man of integrity, honesty, and high standards who does all he can to be accurate in any possible diagnosis or treatment. In short, I have come to trust him.

Over the years that he has been my doctor, he has, on occasion, given me a bad report, that is, a diagnosis that I did not like hearing. His diagnosis was made on the most accurate information he had along with the years of accumulated training and experience that is his in the medical field. He told me the true facts, but I did not like the medical opinion and subsequent conclusions to which he came.

I did *not* call him a liar. I did *not* laugh in his face. I did *not* tell him he was ignorant or that he was way off base. I *did* tell him about my faith in the Lord. I *did* tell him I believed in prayer and the power of faith in Jesus. I *did* tell him I would take whatever corrective or preventive measures he recommended. (You see, we sometimes do things to hurt ourselves and are not fully aware of what we are doing until someone with appropriate knowledge tells us. This is often true concerning diet and exercise in our society.)

Then upon leaving his office, I was true to my words and did as I said I would do. However, I did not stop there. I immediately went to the Word of God. I examined my covenant with the Father through Jesus Christ as to what was mine and the way things should be. Then I based my belief system on what the Word of God said. What the doctor told me was truth based upon natural knowledge. But what the Word of God tells me is a higher level of truth based upon the supernatural power of God to bring to pass in my life all He has said. In short, I got a second opinion, a better opinion.

Even in the natural world, people operate the same way. If the family doctor makes a diagnosis, even he will often recommend a second opinion. Why would he call for a second opinion? If he is a doctor of integrity, he would do so for one of two reasons. One would be as a source of confirmation, that his diagnosis was correct. The other would be to determine that he could have been incorrect in his diagnosis, and things could be far better, or worse, than he originally thought. The point is, he is seeking for the highest and most accurate level of truth upon which to base his diagnosis and future treatment of the patient.

So, when I hear a report that is not what I desire, I always seek a second opinion, a better opinion. And at this writing, after 50 years of ministry and 62 years as a Christian, I can tell you that the opinion of my earthly doctor has always been accurate based on the knowledge he had.

But I can also tell you that the second opinion, the better opinion I have always received from Doctor Jesus has also been accurate, and not only accurate, but was always the opinion I have chosen to receive. Understand, dear reader, that regardless of the level of truth your earthly doctor may possess, the level of truth held by our Lord is higher, and there is one major difference in the truth this world may offer and the truth that comes from the lips of our Messiah.

The difference is the power of fulfillment. The truth of this world has the potential for fulfillment so long as a higher truth does not pre-empt it. But if a higher truth pre-empts a lower truth, the higher truth takes precedent. And please note that the higher truth must pre-empt the lower truth. If the higher truth never comes to light and is never applied, the lower truth will prevail.

The laws of aerodynamics are an example of this. We know that gravity and drag will keep a gigantic air liner on the ground. But if the laws of thrust and lift are known and properly applied with greater force, an aircraft with hundreds of people, their luggage, and fuel, weighing tens of thousands of pounds can rise six or seven miles into the air at 500 mph and cross oceans, non-stop. Now that is amazing. How much more amazing should it be that the law of God's faith can overcome and cancel every natural law that could steal, kill, destroy, or prevent the child of God from achieving the call of God in his life?

Let me encourage you, my dear reader friend, to always seek for the highest possible level of truth, bring yourself to the light of that truth, and apply that truth above all other levels of truth in your life. And know, too, that the highest possible level of truth to which a person can turn and to which that person can hold is the Word of God, the Bible. Hebrews 1:3 says God is "upholding all things by the Word of His power." Jeremiah 1:12 says God "hastens His Word to perform it." John 15:7 declares "if you abide in Me [Jesus], and My Word abides in you, you shall ask what you will, and it shall be done unto you." 1 John 5 speaks of a confidence level in the Lord that is so high that anything we ask according to His will, He does it. And furthermore, you *know* He hears you.

My friend, it doesn't take an enormous amount of study to learn what God's will is concerning your healing and your health. Read 3 John 2, Isaiah 53:4-5, 1 Peter 2:24, Psalm 107:20, Psalm 103:1-3, and Matthew 8:17. Add to that Proverbs 4:20-23 and your foundation for believing the highest possible level of truth begins to build rapidly. Go to the Word for your highest truth, dear reader. You who need healing in your body, go to God's Word. Regardless of all other reports you have received or ever will receive, go to God's Word. Allow that Word to enlighten your heart and mind. Walk in obedience to it. The Word that God has magnified above all His Name will bring you to health and stand in the place of any lower truth.

There is no doubt about it. God's Word is the second opinion so many people need. It is certainly a better opinion than the world can offer, and ultimately can be the only one you really need. The best life is to make God's Word *always your first opinion!*

CHAPTER THREE

A Healed Man Battling Symptoms

Think of this. Since the United States declared, fought for, and won its independence from England, it has been a free nation. In the Revolutionary War, men who wanted to be free fought for their freedom. Since that war, the United States military has never again fought for the freedom of its members and the citizens of the nation they serve. Rather, since the Revolutionary War, United States military personnel have fought to defend, keep, and continue to enjoy the freedoms that became theirs through their victory in the Revolutionary War.

Freedom may still be in the equation of a United States soldier entering into combat, but the truth is that the soldier is already free. They possess freedom, though they may have to fight to preserve it. They are no longer fighting to get it, but for the privilege of continuing to enjoy what is already their possession.

It is the same with healing for the child of God. In the eyes of God, His people are already healed. He has declared it so. So, when sickness or disease comes, the believer is not fighting to get something new, but is instead fighting to keep and see fully manifest what already belongs to him. The reality of what we see is a healed man (or woman) battling symptoms that would prevent him from enjoying what already belongs to him.

Romans 4:17

. . . even God,
who quickeneth the dead,
and calleth those things
which be not
as though they were.

Mark 11:22-24

And Jesus answering saith unto them, Have faith in God. For verily I say unto you, That whosoever shall say unto this mountain, Be thou removed, and be thou cast into the sea; and shall not doubt in his heart, but shall believe that those things which he saith shall come to pass; he shall have whatsoever he saith.

Therefore I say unto you, What things soever ye desire, when ye pray, believe that ye receive them, and ye shall have them.

Romans 3:4

God forbid: yea, let God be true, but every man a liar; as it is written, That thou mightest be justified in thy sayings, and mightest overcome when thou art judged.

Imagine for a moment the following scenario.

A lady patient is sitting quietly in a doctor's office waiting to be called. A nurse calls her name and ushers her into a conference room, making her as comfortable as possible. The doctor enters, greets the lady and her husband, sits down, and opens the medical folder before him. He comes quickly to the point and says, "Mrs. _____, I'm sorry to have to tell you this, but the diagnosis is breast cancer.

It would be impossible to guess how many hundreds, or perhaps thousands of times each year that different women across the globe hear similar statements. And this is only one scenario of one type of cancer. Try to imagine the shock of hearing such news, or being told you have been stricken with some other life-threatening malady. Perhaps you have been one of those people who had to hear such news. And it could be just as devastating to hear that your spouse, or your child, or your parent has been stricken with some debilitating or life-threatening illness. The shock must surely be horrific. The thoughts could assault your mind with the rapidity of machine gun fire. Lives are about to be changed forever. The future has been irrevocably altered. What can you do? To whom can you turn for the answers you need to help you keep on going?

Think, too, of how devastating a diagnosis could be simply due to related medical bills, lost work time, or extended pay loss, and especially to the immediate family. Where would this person turn for help?

If you will remember in the previous chapter, I wrote of a second opinion, a better opinion. Well, here is a marvelous time to remind you of the need for a second opinion. Again, I reiterate that you would be very foolish to simply discount a sound medical opinion from a competent doctor, particularly a specialist in some field. He has given you the most thorough examination possible. He has used his training, education, and every tool at his disposal to correctly assess your medical condition. He has applied all the knowledge he has to concluding what the best course of medical treatment might be. And having done all this, he sometimes feels totally helpless in the face of many sicknesses, diseases, and injuries in our world today. To ignore such knowledge, expertise, wisdom, training, and skill is, quite frankly, stupid.

However, on the other hand, is it not just as *stupid* to ignore a second opinion, particularly if it is a better opinion? And what if that better opinion is from a higher source of truth than the first? Once again, do not ignore the first opinion, particularly if it is from an individual you have no reason to mistrust. But rather use the better opinion as a foundation for building hope in a brighter possible future, and strong faith for a definitely better outcome.

So, what do I do when my doctor, a Christian doctor whom I trust, tells me I have an illness or disease; that I am sick? And what do I do if my doctor tells me I have an incurable disease? Do I immediately go about repeating all my doctor has said to everyone I see? Do I immediately buy into the medical facts my doctor has discovered?

And the answer to all those questions is a resounding, "No!" (And here, dear reader, I write from experience.) Instead, I take a purely Biblical, Scriptural approach to what I have heard. I deal with the words that have been spoken about me in the same way

Jesus did those words spoken to Him at the tomb of Lazarus. (And dear reader friend, if you expect to walk in the highest victories in this life, this is the way to deal with every word that comes into your hearing, not just those that deal with health.)

The first thing I do is realize that my doctor is dealing with a natural level of truth and not a lie in its own right. I accept his findings as factual as the natural world sees and understands them. Then I take those words and place them under the scrutiny of the light of the glorious Word of the living God. In my own personal spiritual growth, I already know what God's Word says about that physical situation, but I still go to His Word to give verifiable credence of what is written there. I find those passages of Scripture that speak of the deliverance the Lord has already provided to me as it relates to my healing and health. I find those passages in the Word that refer to my healing as an already accomplished promise of God for anyone who will believe, confess it, and receive it. I begin immediately to feed my faith that should already be strong. I feed my faith on the only thing that will increase my faith, and that is the Word of God. I apply my faith to the written Word of God that is forever settled in heaven; to the Word that He has magnified above all His name, over which He hastens to perform it; and to the Word that will never return to Him void, but will accomplish that which He pleases and prosper in the thing He sent it to do. I read and quote and listen to the Word that builds my faith; the Word that He sent to heal me and deliver me from my destructions.

And in all that, what do I see? I see a very clear second opinion, and I must say, an eternally better one. My Christian doctor has given his most accurate and honest diagnosis and assessment of what I am facing. But my Doctor Jesus speaks of a prognosis greater than the diagnosis, a different assessment, and in the case of incurable disease, a totally different outcome.

In my 72 years of living (at this writing), I have discovered that if someone wants something badly enough, they will usually do whatever they must in order to have it or acquire it. The same is true with healing and health. I know what my doctor has said. He is a good man. He is an honest man. He is a highly educated and trained man. He is a highly respected man. He is a Christian man. But I also know what my Lord has said, and my doctor being a Christian man, what His Lord has said, too.

My Christian doctor said, "Reverend Moorefield, you are a diabetic, and this is what you need to do." But my Doctor Jesus said, "Himself took my infirmities and bore my sicknesses" (Matthew 8:17), and "by His stripes I was healed" (1 Peter 2:24), and "if you will walk free from diabetes, this is what you must do."

My Christian doctor told me I needed to modify my diet to a healthier one. He was correct. He told me I needed a more regular vigorous exercise program in my routine. He was correct. He told me I needed to have regular times of rest. He was correct. He told me certain types and levels of stress were not good for me. He was correct. Was his diagnosis incorrect? No! Were his recommendations useless? No! And in fact, I have taken them to heart. But when he told me there was no cure for diabetes, and that for the rest of my life I would have to live with it, I drew the line.

Yes, my Christian doctor can surely tell me what is, but he can only guess about what will be. On the other hand, my Doctor Jesus tells me to "call things that be not as though they were."

Well, what was not? Obviously, health was not. So, I took to heart my Christian doctor's diagnosis and advice. At the same time, I held strongly to my profession of faith without wavering, knowing He is faithful that promised. And just how long will I hold fast my profession of faith and call things that be not as though they were? Until they are! And then I will testify of it forever!

I have chosen to believe the highest level of truth as it touches me in every arena of my life. And how does that affect me physically? Well, here's the scenario as it plays out in my life.

I have a Christian doctor who says, "You are a diabetic." I have a Doctor Jesus Who says, "You are healed." Knowing then that my Christian doctor only sees the temporal, but that my Doctor Jesus sees the eternal, the unseen, I choose to hold to the elements of truth that both have spoken that can be reconciled together. And that is this: I am a healed man battling diabetic symptoms.

The symptoms are real, but so is my healing. I have received my healing, and having done so by faith. I now battle the symptoms with that same faith. I have found it much easier to battle symptoms when I know I am healed, than to battle them believing I am sick. In fact, to battle the symptoms, all the while believing I am sick, is utterly futile. Knowing deep within my heart that I am the healed helps me battle the symptoms with a whole different perspective. Knowing the disease is already conquered makes battling symptoms a winnable quest. By faith, I start by winning the war, and then daily taking the battles that come one at a time. Knowing I am the healed enables me to cast all my care on the Lord, daily living the victory that overcomes the world, even my faith.

CHAPTER FOUR

Binding the Strong Man

Matthew 12:25-29

And Jesus knew their thoughts, and said unto them, Every kingdom divided against itself is brought to desolation; and every city or house divided against itself shall not stand:

And if Satan cast out Satan, he is divided against himself; how shall then his kingdom stand?

And if I by Beelzebub cast out devils, by whom do your children cast them out? therefore they shall be your judges.

But if I cast out devils by the Spirit of God, then the kingdom of God is come unto you.

Or else how can one enter into a strong man's house, and spoil his goods, except he first bind the strong man? and then he will spoil his house.

Matthew 16:19

And I will give unto thee the keys of the kingdom of heaven:
and whatsoever thou shalt bind on earth
shall be bound in heaven:
and whatsoever thou shalt loose on earth
shall be loosed in heaven.

Matthew 18:18

Verily I say unto you,
Whatsoever ye shall bind on earth
shall be bound in heaven:
and whatsoever ye shall loose on earth
shall be loosed in heaven.

Luke 10:19

Behold, I give unto you power
to tread on serpents and scorpions,
and over all the power of the enemy:
and nothing shall by any means hurt you.

Mark 16:17

And these signs shall follow them that believe;
In my name shall they cast out devils . . .

Please read closely the passage of Scripture that opens this chapter (Matthew 12:25). Observe the words "every kingdom." It means exactly what it says. "Every kingdom" divided against itself is in a mode of failing, falling apart, coming to naught, and breaking down.

Then note the words "every. . .house" in verse 25. The meaning is still the same. Now I remind you of the words of Paul the Apostle; "What! Know ye not that your body is the temple of the Holy Ghost?" (1 Corinthians 6:19) As I understand it, the temple of Holy Spirit is the same as the true house of God. Well, my friend, if your body is the house of God, and if in your body there is division between what your spirit man knows to be the truth and longs to feast upon, and what your head believes because of the influence of your own senses, the conclusion of that matter should be evident, perhaps even painfully so. If your spirit and soul are at odds with one another, your house is divided, and you will find yourself at a place of inability to stand.

Keep in mind that in Ephesians 6, we are admonished to stand, and more than that, to do all that is necessary to stand. But how can you stand when your spirit and soul are divided within your body, which is the temple of Holy Ghost? The fact is, you cannot. If you will stand, not only must you have on the whole armor of God, you must also be in a house undivided, that is, a place where your soul and spirit are linked together in faith and thinking according to the Word of God. That means having your spirit-man filled to overflowing with the Word of God, and having your soulish realm, which includes your mind, in a constant state of renewal.

But you might ask, "Is the kingdom of Satan so unified that it can defeat the child of God?" And the answer is "yes" and "no." Where Satan rules, he does so by fear, and forces all those under his rule to abide by his will. In that, there is a degree of unity. However, it should never be the case that Satan can in any way or at any time defeat the child of God. So, how then does he apparently overcome so many believers? The answers in totality to that question are many, but one factor is universally discovered in every case of Satan's attacks in your life. It is found in our opening Scripture for this chapter. The fact is, that in order to spoil a strong man's house, you must first bind the strong man. So many Christians find themselves in the throes of defeat because they are living in a condition of *self-division*.

Still, we have not come to the real subject of this chapter, and that is "Binding the Strong Man." What does this have to do with living in a *Covenant of Health*? It has a great deal to do with it. For if you expect to live in a *Covenant of Health*, you must operate the principle set forth in this chapter; the principle of binding the strong man.

In our opening text, Jesus said if you expect to spoil the goods and the house of a strong man, you must first bind the strong man. In Matthew 18, referring specifically to spiritual forces of forgiveness and unforgiveness, the Lord said that we can bind on earth whatever has already been bound in heaven, and by doing so, whatever we bind will truly be bound. At the same time, whatever we loose on earth that has already been loosed in heaven will truly be loosed. Simply put, unforgiveness is bound in heaven and unable to operate there, while at the same time forgiveness is loosed in heaven and able to operate at its fullest potential.

Therefore, when we bind unforgiveness out of our own hearts, it is truly bound out of our lives. And when we loose forgiveness within our hearts, it is truly loosed in our lives.

Though some would say this does not apply in other spiritual arenas, all you need to do is back up two chapters to Matthew 16. There Jesus said that we have been given the keys of the kingdom, and whatever we bind or loose is bound or loosed. While Matthew 18 does indeed deal more specifically with forgiveness and unforgiveness, Matthew 16 opens the field wide for much more. It is in fact all-inclusive for every place of authority in which the Lord has set you by His covenant. If His covenant says you have the authority, you have it. If His covenant says you can do it, you can do it. If His covenant says you possess it, you possess it, whether you see it or not. This is living faith.

Now let us move more directly into the primary subject of this chapter. In order for you to live out a covenant of health, you must learn this principle of binding the strong man. So, first of all, let's determine who the strong man is. The strong man in your life is the individual to whom you bow yourself as having authority in your life in any particular arena. It is that individual to whom you bow to his ability to lord it over you, and have dominion over all of your life or any particular arena in it.

I personally know Christians who are totally sold out to the Lordship of Jesus Christ. Every arena of their life is yielded to Jesus, and it is therefore Jesus Who is the strong man in their life. In order to stop them, in order to bring them down, in order to spoil their life, you would first have to bind the strong man in their life, and that would mean binding Jesus, for they have made

Him the possessor of their total being. Unfortunately, I know other Christians, born again and even Spirit-filled, who at the first sign of sickness or disease bow their knee to the symptoms. Yes, they are saved, but for whatever the reason, they still allow the enemy of their soul to lord it over them through whatever symptoms may arise. By allowing Satan and his forces to control their lives, they have in essence made him the strong man in their lives.

Remember now the authority our Lord gave us to bind and to loose. Remember that He said, Whatever *you* loose... and whatever *you* bind. The key word here is *you*. The work of binding or loosing the strong man in your life is not only your choice, but it is your responsibility.

The Lord did not say He would bind or loose for you, but that *you* would do the binding and loosing. You see, after all has been said, the issue is really a simple one. The ultimate decision rests with *you*. Who do you want to be the strong man in your life? To whom to do you want to yield your life? The simple facts are these.

If you are not born again, you are definitely under the control of a strong man who will carry you to destruction. No, I am not saying you are demon possessed, or even in danger of such. But the simple fact remains, if you don't belong to Jesus, that only leaves one being to whom you can belong.

If you are born again, and your head and your heart are at odds with one another, your house is divided. If your house is divided, there is a strong man that *must* be bound, or he will keep you divided, and will be continually bringing hurt and destruction to your life. And it will seem you are never able to overcome life's battles.

If you are born again, your head and your heart in agreement, and you are serving the Lord Jesus Christ, there is still a strong man in your life, but you don't want to bind Him. You want to make sure this strong man remains loose to work in your life according to His good pleasure.

If you are born again with your head and your heart at odds with one another, I have a solution for you. Bind the strong man! If you don't, you will never be able to enjoy the deepest of the Lord's blessings for you in this earth. How do you bind the strong man? Exercise the spiritual force of the faith of God that is in your heart, speak the Word of God, and if need be, have a saint who is strong in the Lord agree with you. Then step out in faith and begin in earnest the work of renewing your mind by the Word of God. And one more thing; make yourself accountable to a strong mentor in the faith who will help you in your daily walk to keep that strong man bound.

If you are not born again, I have the only solution for you, too. Go to Romans 10:9-10, read it for yourself, and then confess it out loud. Simply put, it says that if you will confess with your mouth the Lordship of Jesus, and believe in your heart that God has raised Him from the dead, you shall be saved.

There are those who would want you to believe this is too simple. Well, they're just wrong. I did not write Romans 10:9-10, and I am glad I did not. But one thing is for sure. I believe Romans 10:9-10, and know it to be the infallible Word of God. Unlike too many churches in our world today who make it *hard* to get in and *easy* to get out, our Lord made it *easy* to get in and a lot *harder* to get out than many would admit or even think.

But just what does praying and confessing Romans 10:9-10 do for the unbeliever concerning the strong man in their life? When a person prays that prayer of confession, it is the very power of God that binds the old strong man in that life, casts him down beneath the Savior's feet, and brings about the new birth. The true strong man in that life is now Jesus.

Now the question arises, "Just what does this have to do with health?" In one sense of the word, everything. Sickness and disease are often, not always, but often the result of a direct demonic attack upon the believer's life. Always remember that the devil comes only to steal, kill, and destroy. When he attacks with sickness and disease, and that attack is not dealt with powerfully and quickly, it can become a stronghold in the believer's body. Given enough time, it will dramatically affect the way the mind and thinking deal with it. Such a stronghold is nothing but the dwelling place of another strong man. Once again, bind the strong man so you can spoil his house!

Simply put, that means you must take authority over the devil who is trying to destroy you. Once you have done this, you can now begin to deal far more effectively with the sickness or disease that has become little more than a hiding place for the destroyer in your life. Sicknesses and diseases are nothing more than houses for the destroyer in a person's life. Bind the strong man; then spoil his house. And just how does one bind that strong man? How do you take authority over such a seemingly awesome foe as the devil? *You* do it by faith with the Word of God coming from *your* lips in the Name of Jesus, *your* Lord.

CHAPTER FIVE

Whose House Is It Anyway?

Regardless of the domicile in which you live, whether you rent, are purchasing, or own it outright, that is your legal dwelling. You, your family, and anyone you may legally designate are the only ones who have free legal entry into your dwelling place. As a rule, anyone else may enter legally only if they have your permission. To do so would be considered trespassing, and if that trespass was forced in some way, it would not only be unlawful entry, but breaking and entering. Whether you call it trespassing, illegal entry, or breaking and entering, it is a violation of the law. In such cases, the resident of that dwelling, has a right to defend himself, his family, any other legal occupants, and his property. The right arises because whether a renter, purchaser, or owner, the place he lives is legally his house.

You live in your body. While, as a child of God, you belong to the Lord, your body is still recognized as your legal residence as long as you live. No one, I repeat, no one, has the right to enter without your permission.

I Corinthians 6:19-20

What? know ye not that your body
is the temple of the Holy Ghost
which is in you,
which ye have of God,
and ye are not your own?
For ye are bought with a price:
therefore glorify God in your body,
and in your spirit,
which are God's.

Imagine the following scenario. A man and his wife arrive home from an evening of dining, and upon their entry, find a burglar working his way through their home. A friend is due at the home any moment to drop off their children she has been babysitting. Instead of running away when he hears the homeowners entering, the burglar assumes a threatening posture that requires the husband to respond in a manner to prevent injury to his wife and himself.

Would this homeowner apologize for intruding on the burglar and politely ask him to leave? Would this homeowner stand idly by as the burglar assaulted him and his wife? Would this homeowner and his wife remain silent as the babysitter comes unexpectingly into the house, bringing herself and their children into grave danger? The answer to all these questions is a resounding "*No!*"

I can assure you that if I were that husband, the person in the greatest danger in my home would not be my wife, my children, the baby-sitter, or myself. The person in the gravest danger of life and limb would be the thief who has broken into *my* house to steal *my* possessions and place *my* family in danger. And while I would not take lightly the stealing of prized possessions from my home, I would in *no* way tolerate threats to my family.

How can a man of God, a minister of the Gospel, say such things? I am sure that many who read this would simply think a minister of the Gospel should always be a man of peace. The Scripture does tell me to live in peace with all men "as much as lieth within me." However, that line is drawn when my family or loved ones are put in danger. Then I will do whatever I must to provide for their maximum security. And this is especially true when it is in my house, on my turf, where I am responsible for provision and safety.

The true believer should have a similar spiritual mindset for his Christian walk in the earth. You see, you are a spirit, you have a soul, and you live in a body. Your body is not only the temple of Holy Ghost, but is also the earthly house for your spirit and soul.

The next point for you to consider is that you have a very real enemy of your soul whose name is Satan. According to John 10:10, while Jesus is come to give you abundant life, the thief, Satan, is come to steal, kill, and destroy anything and everything in your life that you hold dear, and that includes your own life.

So, your body is the place of residence for you and your Lord. There you live together with Jesus. The property is His, yet you are a tenant in common, that is, sharing all the elements of the living quarters, your body. More than that, as His subject, you have been given the power of attorney in His Name to be in charge of the residence. That means you become liable to the owner for the condition of the domicile in which you reside and over which you preside. And once again, that is your body.

Now imagine that a thief is attempting to break in upon your house and destroy it. Are you going to simply allow such a thing to happen, or will you determine to resist the intruder with your whole being and with every legal weapon you have at your disposal? Since you are the one who is currently responsible for the condition of your domicile, the answer is obvious. Since you will ultimately answer to the Lord for what you did to or allowed to happen to your body, you will fight to save it.

The beautiful thing about such a decision is that the decision to fight, when it is a decision of faith, calls on your Lord to assist you by whatever means He must in order to make your resistance a success. In fact, the Scripture plainly states, "submit yourself unto the Lord, resist the devil, and he will flee from you." Keep in mind, your body belongs to the Lord and you are His agent for the business conducted in it. When you are acting as the Lord's agent in the care, attention, and defense of His property, He will fully support you with every needed resource for your success. His assistance means your resistance will be successful.

Such thinking may seem to oversimplify the realities of life in the battle against sickness and disease. However, the fact is that religious thinking that has been embalmed with doubt and unbelief has only served to complicate the simple truth and intent of God's Word. God said what He meant and meant what He said. Accept His Word as absolute truth and act on it in faith.

It is when the believer acts in faith that a pleased Father responds in grace through faith to meet the need and give victory in His child's life. And that victory includes healing from every disease. Regardless of the tool or weapon the enemy would use against you in this life, regardless of what name it is given, including all manner of sickness or disease, your heavenly Father will assure you victory if your will submit yourself to Him and then resist the enemy.

Whose house is it? The house, your body, dear believer, belongs to the Lord. You are a tenant in common with Him, and He has given you power of attorney. You live in your body as though it were your own. Don't allow the thief to steal your health, strength, and life. Yield to your Lord, resist your enemy with all your heart, and keep your house free from destruction. Occupy your house with all diligence through faith, prayer, the Word, and the blood of Jesus.

One more thing. When Jesus said, "In My Father's house are many mansions," He was not talking about heaven, but rather the body of Christ. It's up to you to make your house what you will. Make it a mansion and guard it as such. Allow me a moment to clarify this statement. First, look at the words of Jesus in their context in John 14:2-3. We read . . .

> In My Father's house are many mansions: if *it were* not *so*, I would have told you. I go to prepare a place for you. And if I go and prepare a place for you, I will come again, and receive you unto myself; that where I am, *there* ye may be also.

In examining these verses, consider three words; "house," "mansions," and "place."

HOUSE. Jesus used the term "Father's house." The word "house" is the Greek word "oikia," and it refers to "an inhabited edifice," "the inmates of a house," and "family." Using these definitions as found in Strong's Exhaustive Concordance of the Bible, that term might just as well be rendered as "Father's inmates of the house," or "family." Think of that; Jesus saying, "In My Father's family….."

MANSIONS. The term "mansions" is from the Greek word "monay." According to Strong's Exhaustive Concordance of the Bible, it means "abiding place," and metaphorically speaking, it refers to "Holy Spirit indwelling believers." Wow! What a powerful image. At this point, John 14:2 could then be rendered, "In My Father's family are many believers being indwelled by Holy Spirit." Now imagine that being what Jesus called "mansions."

PLACE. Once again prepare your mind for a marvelous awakening to things yet to come. Jesus said He was going to "prepare a place for you." The word "place" is the Greek word "topos." Once again, according to Strong's Exhaustive Concordance of the Bible, it means a "portion, or space marked off; an inhabited place; a city," or "a place in a book," or "a space limited by occupancy." At this point, using the tools of study available to us to give the clearest possible meaning to Jesus' words in John 14:2, we can see that Jesus was saying, "In My Fathers *house* (family) are many *mansions* (many believers being indwelled by Holy Spirit). I go to prepare a *place* (space marked off for your inhabitance and a space in a book) for you." Oh, what a marvelous picture that paints for each and every member of the Church!

And to add to the completeness and power of that imagery, let us examine 2 Timothy 2:20-21.

> 20 But in a great house there are not only vessels of gold and of silver, but also of wood and of earth; and some to honour, and some to dishonour.
>
> 21 If a man therefore purge himself from these, he shall be a vessel unto honour, sanctified, and meet for the master's use, *and* prepared unto every good work.

Do you remember the Greek word for "house" we saw in John 14:2. It was "oikia." Here in 2 Timothy 2:20, the Greek word for "house" is the same word; "oikia." Therefore, it has the same meaning. It is the Father's "family." Father's house is a great house, and in His house, His "family," there are all kinds of "vessels." But note closely verse 21. "If a man purge himself....

he shall be a vessel unto honour…." To see more clearly what it is from which one should "purge himself," read 2 Timothy 2:14-26. The believer holds awesome power in his own hands, heart, and mouth to become what the Lord desires him to be. When we become that "vessel unto honour," we become one of those "mansions" in and through which the power, glory, majesty, and will of God becomes clearly manifest.

If your name is written in the Book of Life, Jesus left this earth to prepare a place at the marriage supper of the Lamb for the habitation of those who are children of Father (family) and temples of Holy Ghost (mansions) where we may sup with Him, enjoying the marriage supper as we prepare for the coming millennial reign of Christ.

With that description, I ask the question set forth in the title of this chapter. Whose house is it anyway? And since your body is the temple of Holy Ghost, the dwelling place of Father and Son, and you are co-occupants with Him, what will be your response when sickness or disease attempts, by any means, to gain entry into that temple? At any such attempted breach of your spiritual security in the Lord, it would seem that every Biblical safety measure could be employed. Your body is, after all, the temple of our indwelling God. Draw nigh to God and He will draw nigh to you. Resist the devil and he will flee from you. Curse the fig tree. Move the mountain. Speak forth life from a tongue that has the authority to do so. Call things that be not as though they are. Apply Mark 11:22-24. Be a doer of the Word and not a hearer only. Make sure you are fully clad in the whole armor of the Lord, and having done all, to stand, stand. Your body is the house of God in which you co-habit with Him. Defend it!

CHAPTER SIX

The Cure Is Already There

Have you ever been looking for something, perhaps in a drawer or on a particular shelf, but simply could not find it? And then, possibly after going out and buying a new whatever-it-was you needed, found the thing you were looking for in the very place you looked for it the first time? Not only can it be humiliating, but you may even wonder if there was a power at work that was beyond natural.

That is the way it is for many believers. They were facing a physical issue, or it could be emotional or financial. They tried all they knew to do in prayer and asking God for the answer, but it seemed it could not be found. Then, at a later time, perhaps after they had learned some additional spiritual truth, they came to the answer, and were so surprised to find that it was right where they thought it was, but could not seem to find it at the beginning.

The healing you need, the cure for the ailment attacking you, the complete deliverance from every symptom you face is already present. It's already here. It's been here for more than 2,000 years. It's time to find it and put it to work in your life.

1 Peter 2:24

Who his own self bare our sins
in his own body on the tree,
that we, being dead to sins,
should live unto righteousness:
by whose stripes ye were healed.

John 14:6

Jesus saith unto him,
I am the way, the truth, and the life:
no man cometh unto the Father,
but by me.

2 Peter 1:2-3

Grace and peace be multiplied unto you
through the knowledge of God,
and of Jesus our Lord,
According as his divine power
hath given unto us all things
that pertain unto life and godliness,
through the knowledge of him
that hath called us to glory and virtue:

Have you ever heard this old adage? "If it had been a snake, it would have bitten me." I heard often as a boy, and even today in some circles. I've even said it myself. When folks said it, they were talking about searching for something that was very close to them, within reach, yet they did not see it. Everyone I know has experienced that at some point.

In Luke 15, we see the trilogy of parables about the search for and finding of a lost treasure by its owner. In the parables, they focus is on finding someone who is lost from the Lord. The first parable is about the man who had 100 sheep. One of them strayed from the flock, and the owner left the ninety-nine, safe in the fold, while he went out to search for the one that was lost.

The third of the parables is one so familiar to most Christians. It is the parable of the prodigal son. A man had two sons, and the younger called for his inheritance, went away, squandered it, and returned home penniless and ragged to a waiting, loving father who was so grateful for the return of his son.

It is the second parable, found in Luke 15:8-10, to which I bring your focus for a moment. It is about the woman who had ten pieces of silver, and having lost one of the pieces in the house, she cleaned the house thoroughly, searching diligently for it until she found it. Once again, the meaning is not lost, nor should it be. But I point to this parable for it speaks to my opening statement. The lost piece of silver was not lost outside the house, nor was it removed from the house to a far-away place. It was in the house, at times during the woman's search, no doubt very close to her. It was her possession, and at times she may have been within inches of it, but did not see it until she searched diligently. There is a lesson to be learned here.

So often in life, the thing we need, the thing we so strongly desire, is, as another old adage says, "right under our nose." It is so close we can touch it, but not being seen (perceived by our senses), it may as well be on the other side of the world. This can be frustrating, confusing, even embittering, but where our healing and health is concerned, this should not be the case. Still, too often, it is, and sadly so. Healing (health) belongs to the believer. It has been fully produced, purchased, and provided to us by the redemptive work of Jesus. It is the possession of the believer. It belongs to everyone who is a member of the body of Christ. It is a vital part of our redemptive blessing, right, and even responsibility.

Yet there are so many members of the body of Christ, while being rightful owners of healing and health, cannot lay hold on it for themselves, for they have lost it somewhere in the house. At that point, there needs to be a thorough house cleaning. Something in their house, in their life, is keeping a precious possession provided by our Lord, hidden from them. If it is sin, it needs to be removed from the house. Jesus has provided the act of confession of our sin (1 John 1:9) and His blood for that cleansing. It may be tradition. Our Lord has provided the Scriptures for us to utilize in obedience to Romans 12:2 for the renewing of our minds so traditions no longer blind us to our possession. It could be ignorance of the Word of God, for which, once again, the Lord has provided His Word (Proverbs 4:20-23) and Holy Spirit (John 16:13), along with the church and the five-fold ministry (Ephesians 4:11-12) so we can learn, grow, and become strong and victorious in Christ. With these tools in hand, we can find the healing and health that belongs to us, and rejoice in its finding. Without them we remain, as some would say, in the dark. And there, in the darkness, in our own house where light should rule, is where the enemy of your soul works to keep you. And in that same darkness is the treasure we desperately need, and for which we should be searching.

Don't misunderstand my following words as cruel. I merely share them as an example of what I say. A person who is completely blind learns to live in that state of darkness, and many live as normal a life as possible. And if something happens that all the lights go out, and where the blind person is becomes completely dark, he/she will likely do quite well. They are accustomed to working without light. But a sighted person would most likely be in immediate trouble, possibly even very afraid, for they are *not* accustomed to working in the dark. So it is for Christians who attempt to live some part, or most of their lives in spiritual darkness when they have been designed to see and function in the light. When they choose, or are deceived, to live in darkness, they must bear up under great difficulties.

Allow me to give you another example, a personal one. I was born again at age 10 on June 17, 1959, in a small Baptist church in Pinnacle, North Carolina. We had a wonderful pastor. My dad worked at nights, so on Wednesday nights, the pastor and his wife would come and take my mother and me to church with them. For them, it was a total drive of about 25 miles, one way. On Wednesday evenings, after church, if there were church folks who were sick and wanted prayer, the pastor would drive to their house and pray for them before returning home. When the pastor, his wife, and my mother would go into a house to pray for someone, I would stay in the car, and pray on my own. Often my prayers, even as a child, were so strong, deep, and fervent that I could be found weeping for those for whom I was praying. There were times I reached a point when I did not have the words to say, and I would hear groanings coming from within me. I did not know then, for I was young and completely untaught, how close I was to receiving the infilling of Holy Spirit with the initial physical evidence of speaking in tongues as Holy Spirit gave utterance. You see, being untaught, untrained, and so very ignorant of many spiritual things, I did not know that Holy Ghost baptism belonged to me. In fact, I didn't even know such a thing existed.

I really do understand what it means to be a possessor of a great blessing, but not even be aware that I possess it, how to lay hold of it, or how to receive the benefits of it. The truly sad part of the story is that over time, not realizing such a great blessing was mine, and not accessing or experiencing it, I grew content to live without what I did not know was mine. Oh, how thankful I am for the God Who loves me, and the wife He gave me. My bride had grown up in the home of a Church of God minister, and was very familiar with the work and ministry of Holy Ghost. So, after our marriage, we attended a local Church of God. It was there that I learned what I had been so close to as a lad, and it was there that I first tasted of that wonderful gift. My life was changed forever. That precious possession that was hidden in the darkness of my ignorance came to light, I took hold of it, and have not released it from my life since that day. For many people today, healing and health fall into that same example. It belongs to every believer, but because of ignorance, tradition, or garbage in their lives, that marvelous gift of God is hidden from them. I pray this writing helps many to find it.

Healing and health, my friend, belongs by covenant to every child of God. Isaiah 53:4-5 stated it in the present tense. Psalm 107:20 stated it in the past tense of God's work to Israel when they would cry out to Him, and Malachi 3:6 declares God changes not. Matthew 8:17 shows His will in the healing of Peter's mother-in-law, and states it in the past tense saying, "Himself took our infirmities and bear our sicknesses." Psalm 103:2-3 declares Father's will and desire to heal and keep in health as an ongoing work of God for His people, saying, "Bless the Lord, O my soul, and forget not all His benefits. Who forgives all your iniquities; Who heals all your diseases." And let us not forget 1 Peter 2:24 that states from a completely New Covenant perspective, "Who His Own Self bare our sins in His Own body on the tree, that we, being dead to sins, should live unto righteousness: by Whose stripes ye were healed." Note that in New Testament verbiage, our healing is set forth as a past tense action. It is already done. The cure for the believer is not yet to come, nor is it coming. *The cure is already there.* And where is "there?" "There" is in covenant, in His Word, in your life, in God's house, in the Church, *in you!*

CHAPTER SEVEN

Fighting to Keep What You Already Have

I believe that I am a kind, gentle, loving, and giving human being. All these are things I have learned from the Lord and those He has set about me in my life. They are likewise characteristics of my Heavenly Father Who has set His spiritual DNA into my being when I was born again of the incorruptible seed of the Word of God.

One of the things I have seen in my Father, and that I also know exists in me, is knowing that there are some things worth the fight to keep. God is perfect in all His ways, and can in no way lie or be defeated. I am yet human, and while I do have the divine nature of God in me as His son, I am often in a place where I not only must fight the good fight of faith, but must also make a discerning choice of whether something is worth the fight to keep. My faith is one of those things for which the Lord has commanded me to contend, or fight. There are other things, too, for which I will contend. My bride, my family, my family in Christ, and those blessings the Lord has given me to use for His kingdom. I will not stand by and watch them stolen or destroyed. For them, I will fight, and I will fight to win.

1 Kings 21:3

And Naboth said to Ahab,
The LORD forbid it me,
that I should give
the inheritance of my fathers
unto thee.

2 Peter 1:3

According as his divine power
hath given unto us all things
that pertain unto life and godliness,
through the knowledge of him
that hath called us to glory and virtue:

Ephesians 6:10-11

Finally, my brethren,
be strong in the Lord,
and in the power of his might.
Put on the whole armour of God,
that ye may be able to stand
against the wiles of the devil.

In the years of my pre-pastoral and early pastoral ministry, I lived in a place where I could have a garden. We were in the country with about an acre of land. I really enjoyed having my garden. It was beautiful, especially when it was lush and green, and producing fruit abundantly. What a joy it was to walk through it and pick fresh vegetables of so many kinds.

But if you know anything about gardening, you know the garden doesn't just happen. You must clear the ground of many obstacles. While according to the Scriptures, the ground wants to please you, there are weeds, briars, thorns, and rocks that are content to remain where they are, hinder your work, and choke out anything you plant.

But clearing the ground alone is not enough. You must plow the ground, and then break up the plowed ground into a finer mix of soil into which you can sow your seed. Add to that the need to organize your garden into rows or beds, sowing in an orderly manner that which you desire to harvest. All this laborious and time-consuming work must be accomplished *before* you see the beginning of fruit. And let us not forget the labor of harvesting. There are times the work seems endless.

Sometimes in that process of making a beautiful garden, one must also wait. When you sow the seed, you don't have immediate fruit. When you fertilize, you don't have immediate growth. When you water, you don't see and immediate increase in the volume of fruit. With each of those tasks comes a time of waiting, or as the Scriptures say, the husbandman waits patiently for the harvest. And during those times of waiting, there is tending, or giving one's attention to other work involved with gardening. Allow me to relate an incident to you about what can happen in waiting.

In the early 1980's, while living where I could have a large garden, I was in my third year of gardening. In the third year, I did not have to do so much of the hard labor I accomplished in the first two years. That part of the work, being accomplished each year, was getting easier and less time-consuming. The ground was prepared. I had prepared for irrigation, sown my seed in well-laid rows, and almost daily, before seeing even the sprouts of the seeds I had sown, I walked through the garden looking for and removing any weeds, even tiny ones that had sprouted.

During a time of study in the Scriptures, I took a stretch break, and stood for a moment looking out the back door of our home. The garden, though still only looking like a plowed field, created in my mind a wonderful image of fruitfulness. As I looked out the door, I watched a crow fly from a nearby tree and land at the edge of my garden. He walked leisurely past each row, glancing down that row for a moment. When he came to my first row of recently planted corn, he stopped, turned toward that row, and prepared to enter my garden and feast on the, as yet, unemerged seedlings. It was as if he had radar to pick out the corn rows.

His story ended right there. He died with delusions of grandeur. I shot and killed the crow before he took his first step into my garden. You see, that was *my* garden. I was the one who worked it. I cleared the land. I plowed it. I prepared the soil. I sowed the seed. I fertilized the ground. I watered the soil. I paid for the seed and fertilizer that went into the ground. It was *my* garden. And I was *not* going to allow a thief to steal and destroy my work. In a manner of speaking, I was fighting for what I already had.

This is the way life works when we live by faith. As a child of God, there are things my Father and my Lord has provided me through the redemptive work of Jesus and the New Covenant. Having been provided to me, *they are mine!* They belong to me. Father has given them to me. I don't need to ask for them. I don't need to beg for them. I don't need to pay extra for them. The full price has already been paid, I have the bill of sale in my hand, written and hidden in my heart, and always in my mouth. It is the Word of God.

Some things that many believers call promises are not promises. They are accomplished facts. If I promise to give you something, you do not possess it. On the other hand, if you already possess it, it is *not* a promise. Healing is not a promise. It is a settled conclusion. "By His stripes you were healed" (1 Peter 2:24). Once a person has accepted Jesus as Lord and is born again, all the things that redemption delivers to us belongs to that person. He doesn't have to ask the Lord to be born again; it's already done. They don't have to ask the Lord for the renewing of their mind; they have the tools, so they can go to work for themselves and be guided and led by Holy Spirit. They don't need to ask the Lord for life's necessities; seek first the kingdom of God and His righteousness, and all these things will be added to you. They don't need to ask the Lord for protection; they're already living in Psalm 91 covenant. In each of these examples, what one needs and desires is already a gift given, a fact accomplished, a promise rendered (not waiting to be rendered). All one must do is appropriate that which Father has already given. And never, *never, never* forget to be thankful.

Both healing and health fit in this arena. Jesus has *already* paid the price for your complete redemption. The only part of that full redemption that is waiting to be accomplished is the glorifying of our body when Jesus comes for His church, when the dead in Christ rise first, and we that are alive and remain shall be caught up to be with the Lord. Healing and health have, however, already been purchased, delivered, and rendered to us in the Name of Jesus when we became part of the body of Christ through the new birth.

Yes, I know. The church is absolutely embalmed in some cases with so much tradition that the truth of what I'm writing will either be rejected, ignored, or stumbled over through repeated approach to a promise *fulfilled* as a promise *still pending* the meeting of some obligation. There are those who pray for God to heal if it is His will. 3 John 2 should render such praying a moot point in the church. There are those who believe it is God's will to heal, but approach it as a promise made but not yet rendered. Such an approach is, in truth, unbiblical. Why would a born-again man have to ask God to save his soul? He wouldn't. He is already born again, and the salvation of the soul is part of that work. No, it may not be accomplished in the Christian at the new birth, but every tool and help God has for that work to be accomplished has already been delivered into the life of the believer. One does not need to ask for it, but rather must pick it up and use it.

The simple fact is this. Healing already belongs to the child of God. By the stripes of Jesus, as Father views it, and as He would desire it to be seen in the believer's life, every believer has already been healed. There is nothing for which we need to ask, but there is much for which we need to fight. Healing and health belong to you right now, my friend. There is no longer a need to ask for it.

But to live a life where healing is always manifest when we need it, you will have to fight for it. And to grow beyond that to live a life in which we live in divine health, you will have to fight for it.

But you will never fight for it in that manner until you conclude that it is already your possession, already given to you by the Lord, already precious and treasured in your life, and not something being held back until you ask for it, or something you have yet to earn. It belongs to you *now*! The price for it has already been totally paid. It belongs to you *now*! There is no more that can be done to provide it to you. It belongs to you *now*!

And what makes these statements so powerful is the truth that God has not only given you healing and health, but He has fully equipped, clothed, and armored you to fight for it. Put on the whole armor of God. You don't have to ask for it. It has already been set before you. *Put it on!* Put it on so you can stand against the wiles of the devil. You see, it has been the wiles (the deceptive words, actions, and interference) of the devil that have so many Christians so convinced that healing and health is something the Lord has yet to provide them. Now you know that such thinking is erroneous. Healing and health belong wholly to you. Armor up, and get busy fighting to keep what you already have. You may have to learn how to work this in your life. Holy Spirit will teach you. You *will* have to exercise your faith to walk in it, to simply receive it from God as a present possession, and boldly put yourself forth into the battle without fear, without wavering, and without doubt. You *will* have to defend yourself with the shield of faith to quench all the fiery darts of Satan, for in this arena, the fiery darts are numerous beyond count. But remember, this is the victory that overcomes the world, even your faith.

CHAPTER EIGHT

His Hands Extended

The believer in Christ is a member of the body of Christ. Jesus is the Head and we are the body. The body is made of many members. We all serve one another, working together to serve the work of the Kingdom to accomplish the will of Father. We need one another. No one of us is more needful than any other, but we are all highly needed in the role we have been called to fill. We should each be deeply honored to be a part of the body of Christ. Fill your role; fulfill your duties; complete your assignments; honor the Head; acknowledge your need of one another.

We are all called to lay hands on the sick. To that extent, we are all hands. Some of us may play a greater role in that work than others, but the task belongs to all of us. We need one another. How could the hand work without the fingers, the wrist, the forearm, the elbow, the upper arm, the shoulder? And on and on I could go.

In serving the Kingdom and one another, we all have hands to offer. Open them to grasp that which is needed, to release that which can be given, and to perform that which needs to be done. There must be no doubt – We are His hands extended.

Mark 16:17-18

And these signs shall follow them that believe;
In my name shall . . . .
. . . . they shall lay hands on the sick,
and they shall recover.

1 Corinthians 12:21

And the eye cannot say unto the hand,
I have no need of thee:
nor again the head to the feet,
I have no need of you.

John 14:12-14

Verily, verily, I say unto you,
He that believeth on me,
the works that I do shall he do also;
and greater works than these shall he do;
because I go unto my Father.
And whatsoever ye shall ask in my name,
that will I do,
that the Father may be glorified in the Son.
If ye shall ask any thing in my name,
I will do it.

A wonderful songwriter by the name of Vep Ellis (1917-1988) wrote the following words in a song titled "Let Me Touch Him." It was in the chorus that he penned, "Oh to be His hand extended, reaching out to the oppressed." Such a powerful statement, and yet horribly ignored or misunderstood in much of the 21st century church.

When we read the Epistles of Paul the Apostle, one of the recurring themes is the body of Christ. When Jesus was in the earth in the flesh, He was both the head and body of Christ. But after His resurrection and ascension, and the sending of Holy Spirit on the day of Pentecost, things clearly changed. Now Jesus is seated on the right hand of Father, and He ever lives to make intercession for the saints according to the will of Father. And further, now we have been made to be ambassadors of Christ in the earth (2 Corinthians 5:17-21). We have become the body of Christ (Ephesians 5:23; Colossians 1:18; Colossians 2:19).

With Jesus as the head of the body and the church as the body of Christ, we take our lead from Him. As Isaiah wrote, "the government shall be upon His shoulder" (Isaiah 9:6). Once again, the imagery is clear. The head sits on the shoulders. Jesus, the Head of body, the Church, holds the position of leadership and ultimate oversight over the body of Christ, the Church.

Holding that imagery in your mind, consider how you could live, or what you could accomplish, if all you were was a head. Without a head, the body is dead. Without a body, the head has no mobility, agility, or ability to do what the head desires. As the body of Christ in the earth, we are His mobility to move about in all the world into which we are sent to preach the Gospel. As the body of Christ, we are His agility to carry out His desires and will when He desires it in an expeditious manner. As the body of Christ, we are His ability in the earth to accomplish His plans and will in the world. In Him we live, and move, and have our being (Acts 17:28).

Now let us look further into the relationship between the Head of the body (Jesus, the Christ) and the body (the Church). I have, on a number of occasions, heard ministers make a statement from the pulpit that should never come from the lips of men of God. I have heard ministers tell congregations that in the scheme of things, God really doesn't need them; that He can get along just fine without them. My dear friend, while I fully understand that my absence, or yours, from this earth will not stop the ultimate plan of God, saying that God does not need a member of the body of Christ is a lie. Read the following passage from 1 Corinthians 12:20-23.

> But now *are they* many members, yet but one body. And the eye cannot say unto the hand. I have no need of thee: nor again the head to the feet, I have no need of you.
>
> Nay, much more those members of the body, which seem to be more feeble, are necessary:
>
> And those *members* of the body, which we think to be less honourable, upon these we bestow more abundant honour; and our uncomely *parts* have more abundant comeliness.

The broader point here is that not only do we in the body of Christ need one another, but according to the passage just shared, the Head of the body needs us as well. Did you read the words of verse 21? "And the eye cannot say unto the hand, I have no need of thee: nor again the head to the feet, I have no need of you." Note these words closely. The head *cannot* say to the feet, the furthest removed part of the body from the head, "I have no need of you." That is an awesomely powerful statement. *Every* part of the body is needful to *every other* part of the body, even to the head. And in the case of the body of Christ, the Head is Jesus and believers are all the other parts. Perhaps we should note at this point that one of the great causes for a great lack of the manifest power of God through the body of Christ today may be a result of our failure to recognize the importance of other parts, and in some cases, even a sense of *amputation* of some body parts. Just a thought.

But the focus of this chapter is the hand of the body. Let's look closer. In Mark 16:18, we read that believers shall lay hands on the sick and they shall recover. That should be clearly evident to anyone who can read. We are sent by the Lord to bring healing to the sick, and in particular, the unbelievers. Knowing that it is the will of God for His people to live in health (3 John 2; Proverbs 4:20-23; Psalm 103:1-3; Psalm 107:20), we should take that into account as we read the Mark 16 passage. The focus is:

1. Going into the world. That is to the unsaved.
2. Preaching the Gospel to every creature (that includes the lost).
3. And certain signs following the believer, not performed *for* the believer, but *by* the believer.

Every believer should recognize the powerful truth that God has a work for him to do with his hands – lay them on the sick. Yes, the laying on of hands has other functions in the body of Christ as well. But not every believer is a member of the presbytery, or an elder. But *every* believer has been sent to lay hands on the sick. And what's more, they shall recover.

And yet there is more to consider here, especially when we include what we call *types and shadows* found in the Scriptures. For instance, referring to the church as the body of Christ is an example of that very thing. Another is referencing the church as the bride of Christ. And of course, the Old Testament is filled with examples of types and shadows. Oil is often a type of Holy Spirit. Water is often a type of Holy Spirit, or the Word. One type and shadow often referenced is God's command that one could not eat flesh of an animal that did not chew the cud, or did not have cloven feet (Deuteronomy 14:1-8). I call this the talk-walker doctrine. The animal that chews the cud is a type and shadow of a man of God who keeps the Word of God in his mouth. The animal with the cloven foot is a type and shadow of a man of God who walks in the light of the Word of God. Unless a man of God meets both requirements, he should not be considered a safe source of spiritual food. I know that sounds very restrictive, and it is, but consider this. How many drops of arsenic would I have to put into your bottle of water before you would not drink it? Remember, a little leaven leavens the whole lump (Galatians 5:1-9).

But let us look at one of the most beautiful types and shadows in the Scriptures – the tree, and in particular, a tree with leaves. As a believer, a Christian, one is "a tree of righteousness, the planting of the Lord" (Isaiah 61:1-3). As the trees of righteousness, we are the trees of the field that shall clap their hands when believers go out with joy speaking forth the Word of God that will not return to Him void (Isaiah 55:6-12). And let us not forget that Jesus said of Himself, "I am the vine and you are the branches" (John 15:5). Leaves grow on the branches. And we dare not omit the beautiful imagery of the trees of life on either side of the river that flows from beneath the throne of God. They bring forth 12 manner of fruit each month, and their leaves are for the healing of the nations (Revelation 22:1-2). Such beauty in imagery, and such power in plan and purpose *must not* go unrecognized, and even more important than recognizing it, is living out the mission it paints for every believer in the church.

So, let's put it all together. Jesus is the head of the body of Christ. We, the church, are the body. Jesus holds reign over the church, and it is the responsibility of the church to carry out the desires and plans of our Lord. Jesus wants us rooted by the rivers of water so we can constantly grow and be fruitful in every season of life (Psalm 1:1-3). He is the vine and we, the church, are the branches. It is on the branches that the fruit is born, and it is on the branches that leaves grow. It is in the leaves of a tree that the nourishment and water drawn from the roots are transformed into the food necessary for life in and growth of the tree. Those leaves on the trees of righteousness in the kingdom of God, the Church, are clapped in praise and celebration at the work of the kingdom and the bringing forth of the Word of God.

And we *must not forget*, those leaves are for the healing of the nations. Do you see the picture? The leaves, your hands, my hands, the hands of every Christian carry a divine purpose. That purpose, regardless of any other calling you may have in the body of Christ, is for the healing of the nations. We are the trees of righteousness, the planting of the Lord. Our hands are to be raised in praise to our God. Our hands are for clapping in praise to the

Lord and encouraging those who carry forth the Word of life. Our hands are for laying on the sick in faith according to Mark 16 for the healing of the nations. Our hands are His hands extended.

In Luke 4, the Lord Jesus took the scroll of Isaiah and found what we know as Isaiah 61:1-2. Luke recorded it in this manner.

> The Spirit of the Lord *is* upon me, because he hath anointed me to preach the gospel to the poor; he hath sent me to heal the brokenhearted, to preach deliverance to the captives, and recovering of sight to the blind, to set at liberty them that are bruised, To preach the acceptable year of the Lord.

Did you notice the words "to heal" and "preach deliverance" and "recovering of sight" and "set at liberty them that are bruised"? Each term references healing in some manner. That is one of the key purposes of your hands as a Christian. Wash yourself in the cleansing water of God's Word, fill your heart and mouth with the word of God that was sent to heal and deliver. Open your heart to Holy Spirit Who can direct you as He will to the place where you can carry out the good works you were ordained to do (Ephesians 2:10). And then step out to do that which you have been called and anointed to do . . . to be His hands extended, bringing healing, life, health, and strength to a world so desperately in need of a real relationship with the risen Lord. Go ahead and say it aloud, boldly . . . "My hands are His hands extended, leaves of a tree of righteousness, the planting of the Lord, that He might be glorified." Now go and glorify your Lord.

CHAPTER NINE

Refuse Captivity

I am convinced that in the make-up of man, there is an inherent desire for freedom. I am not talking about a life without rules or laws, but a life in which one is free to pursue happiness, dreams, desires, and wishes in a manner, or manners, that do not injure or bring harm to others, and that do not prevent others from using their legitimate means of doing the same.

Nelson Mandela said, "For to be free is not merely to cast off one's chains, but to live in a way that respects and enhances the freedom of others." When one lives life in this manner, one is not likely at all to accept captivity. It will be resisted, and that strongly so. Such is an absolutely Biblical attitude; a lifestyle that should be that of every Christian.

Christ has made me free. He has redeemed me from the curse of the law. But He has not made me free to hurt, injure, disenfranchise, or diminish others. Where other human beings are concerned, I am to do to them as I wish them to do to me. I am to love them as I love myself. I may not agree with them, or they with me, but I am not free to force my personal will upon them. Just as Christ has made me free, so He wishes freedom for all people. But in all our human interactions, in every place of my life, I will refuse to be captive to anything or anyone other than Jesus Christ, to Whom I am a willing slave.

Psalm 107:20

He sent his word, and healed them,
and delivered them from their destructions.

John 8:31-32

Then said Jesus to those Jews
which believed on him,
If ye continue in my word,
then are ye my disciples indeed;
And ye shall know the truth,
and the truth shall make you free.

Romans 8:1-2

There is therefore now no condemnation
to them which are in Christ Jesus,
who walk not after the flesh,
but after the Spirit.
For the law of the Spirit of life in Christ Jesus
hath made me free from the law of sin and death.

On occasion, over my five decades of ministry, I have received something in the mail or by special delivery for which I had to sign a document indicating that I had received it. I remember once hearing a great man of God ask, "If someone sent a box of rattle snakes to your house, a box you had not ordered, and you knew the snakes were in the box, would you sign for it?" Of course, we know the answer to that query. "No!" In fact, I would not even allow the package to be left at my door. I would handle it by having the legal authorities deal with it in a manner that forced the sender to pay for such a dangerous action.

It should be no different with the believer as it regards *anything* that the enemy of our soul would send to us. *Nothing* that Satan sends to a believer is for good; it is all for evil. The Scriptures declare that Satan comes for nothing but to steal, kill, and destroy. Jesus did not say that some things, or a few things, or something once-in-a-while comes to us from Satan that is in some way a blessing. Again, I urge you to read, meditate upon, and earnestly believe the words of Jesus; "The thief cometh not but for but for to steal, and to kill, and to destroy" (John 10:10). Never allow anything that comes from Satan to deceive you into thinking that it has any good in it at all. It does not!

I know there are many who believe that God uses the devil to teach, or if need be, to correct or chasten the errant Christian. Nothing could be further from the truth. God would never send a thief to steal from a child of God so the child of God would know what it means to have to give something up. God would never send a murderer to teach a child of God how to give life. God would never send a wrecker and destroyer to teach a child of God how to bless and build. That would be like giving a venomous snake to your child as a pet. Regardless of how beautiful the snake seemed to be, or how it might seem to enjoy the warmth of being coiled in one's pocket, sooner or later that viper will do exactly what its nature dictates. It would bite, and when it does, the results would be to steal, kill, and destroy.

Furthermore, everything that comes from Satan for the purpose of stealing, killing, and destroying always works to imprison or enslave someone in the shackles and holding cells of darkness. The child of God must remember that the Christian is in no way designed by our Maker to be a prisoner. Our God wants us to be and live free in Him. How often in the Word of God do we see the work of Satan as that of imprisoning people? Words such as captive, prisoner, slave, snared, trap, entangle, chains, fetters, and the like all indicate being in a place of imprisonment, and they are terms that speak to the devices of Satan to catch, steal, kill, and destroy God's people.

I am amazed at the number of Christians I encounter who spend their whole life as a believer either trying to discover a way out of the captivity that holds them, or seeking a way to avoid the captivity in which they have so often found themselves. It is so sad to see many people who love the Lord existing in captivity after captivity, often the same captivity, and never really living free from any and all captivity.

Now don't misunderstand what I am saying. There is no way of numbering the times I have had an opportunity for captivity offered to me. I can assure you it is daily. I have learned that if I deal with such issues the moment they arise, I won't find myself in a position of needing to be freed from some captivity later. I simply reject them out of hand. That's the way Jesus did it, and we are to be followers (imitators) of Him. If I pattern my day-today living after the manner in which Jesus lived, I don't have to be freed from captivity, but rather I live free.

When I became a believer, I was placed in a new covenant relationship with God. In that new relationship, as a new creature in Christ Jesus, I became the righteousness of God in Christ Jesus. And the moment that happened, I became a recipient of redemption that my Lord provided in His New Covenant. Since that moment of the new birth, I have been redeemed from the curse of the law, Jesus Himself being made a curse for me.

However, at that point in time, I did not know all I do now. Though I was redeemed from that moment forward, a lack of knowledge caused me to think I still lived in the arena of captivity. Wrong teaching in the body of Christ, along with the traditions that had developed through that wrong teaching had me convinced that sickness, disease, lack, even poverty, and many kinds of oppression and depression were tools used by the Lord to keep His people humble.

Ah, but thank the Lord God Almighty for His long-suffering, love, faithfulness, and patience. He kept me, even in the captivity of my ignorance and tradition, until He could show me through His Word how I, too, could be set free, go free, and remain free in Him. And so often He used the actions of men and women of God "who through faith and patience have obtained the promises," to show me how that was possible. Oh, how my heart rejoices in knowing that I am free from every element of the curse of the law.

- **Sin** – Jesus bore my sins in His body on the cross, so that I, being dead to sin, can live unto righteousness – 1 Peter 2:24

- **Sickness** – He sent His Word and healed me – Psalm 107:20; and by His stripes we were healed – 1 Peter 2:24
- **Poverty** – if I walk in and keep His Word, His commandments, He will make my way prosperous and give me good success – Joshua 1:8; it is His highest desire and greatest pleasure that I prosper and live in health – 3 John 2
- **Freedom from Darkness** – the entrance of His Word brings light – Psalm 119:130; His Word is a light unto my path – Psalm 119:105
- **Victory in All Things** – I am the head and not the tail; above only and not beneath; my enemy comes before me one way and flees before me seven ways – Deuteronomy 28:7; and this is the victory that overcomes the world, even my faith – 1 John 5:4

And I could continue in arena after arena of life. As a child of God, I have been made an ambassador of God in this earth. I am to live as a representative of the Lord Jesus Christ in word, deed, character, and practice, modeling the life of a victorious believer.

But perhaps the greatest question that would arise from this writing is, "How can one live such a life? How does one reject captivity?" The answer is truly a simple one, but one that requires knowledge of the Word of God, determination to obey the Word of God, and the faith to speak the Word of God in a manner consistent with the Word Who was made flesh, Jesus Himself.

Take the time to read Matthew 4:1-11. . .

Then was Jesus led up of the Spirit into the wilderness to be tempted of the devil.

And when he had fasted forty days and forty nights, he was afterward an hungered.

And when the tempter came to him, he said, If thou be the Son of God, command that these stones be made bread.

But he answered and said, It is written, Man shall not live by bread alone, but by every word that proceedeth out of the mouth of God.

Then the devil taketh him up into the holy city, and setteth him on a pinnacle of the temple,

And saith unto him, If thou be the Son of God, cast thyself down: for it is written, He shall give his angels charge concerning thee: and in *their* hands they shall bear thee up, lest at any time thou dash thy foot against a stone.

Jesus said unto him, It is written again, Thou shalt not tempt the Lord thy God.

Again, the devil taketh him up into an exceeding high mountain, and sheweth him all the kingdoms of the world, and the glory of them;

And saith unto him, All these things will I give thee, if thou wilt fall down and worship me.

Then saith Jesus unto him, Get thee hence, Satan: for it is written, Thou shalt worship the Lord thy God, and him only shalt thou serve.

Then the devil leaveth him, and, behold, angels came and ministered unto him.

Now having read that passage, let's take a few moments to refer back to it to learn how Jesus lived a life completely rejecting captivity, remembering that this model works in every arena of life, including healing and living in health.

In this passage we see that Jesus had just fasted for 40 days, and was now hungry. That happens naturally when one goes on a protracted fast of this nature. When hunger pangs return late in the fasting period, the body is telling you that if food is not consumed soon, the body will enter into starvation mode and death becomes a threat. That is the stage of the fast to which Jesus had come. It was at this point that Satan came to tempt Him.

The first temptation dealt with that very issue – Jesus's hunger. Satan said, "If thou be the Son of God, command these stones be made bread" (Matthew 4:3). And what was the response of Jesus? He said, "It is written, Man shall not live by bread alone, but by every word that proceedeth out of the mouth of God." (Deuteronomy 8:3; Matthew 4:4)

Then came the second temptation. "If thou be the Son of God, cast thyself down: for it is written, He shall give his angels charge concerning thee: and in *their* hands they shall bear thee up, lest at any time thou dash thy foot against a stone" (Matthew 4:5-6). And again, the Lord's response was, "It is written again, Thou shalt not tempt the Lord thy God." (Deuteronomy 6:16; Matthew 4:7) Do you see any similarity in response? While the Scripture the Lord referenced is different, His lead into His response was identical... "It is written ..."

And again, with the third temptation we see the same lead into response. Satan took Jesus to a high place, showing Jesus the kingdoms of the world and their glory, tempting Him with, “All these things will I give thee, if thou wilt fall down and worship me” (Matthew 4:9). And with this third Satanic attempt, we read Jesus’s response, “Get thee hence, Satan: for it is written, Thou shalt worship the Lord thy God, and him only shalt thou serve.” (Deuteronomy 6:13; Matthew 4:10) And again, this third time, we see the lead-in phrase, “It is written.”

For each of the three temptations, Jesus used different Old Testament passages for rebuttal, or to reject the potential captivity, but in all three, His lead-in was the same phrase; “It is written.” Do you see it? Jesus’s Own rebuttal against anything from Satan that would bring Him into captivity was the Word of God. Jesus, the Word made flesh, had to use the speaking forth of that which was written. He did *not* try to use human reasoning in any form, or even to use words of His own choosing. In order to wield authority over His enemy, Jesus chose the only weapon that would work to defeat Satan completely – the Word of God spoken from the lips of a son of God in full faith. And that is precisely what Jesus did. And as one translation declares, when Jesus had so answered the devil, Satan left Jesus for a more convenient time, which of course, he never found.

CHAPTER TEN

Holy C.P.R.
(Don't Let Death Leave Samples)

My older grandson has been trained as an EMT (emergency medical technician). I am proud of him. The knowledge he carries within his mind, the will to serve and help others, and his ability to transfer that knowledge and will through his hands to doing actual life-saving services for other human beings is, in my thinking, a truly awesome thing.

One of the skills he has acquired, and which must be maintained to continue in his work, is the knowledge and skill to apply the knowledge of CPR (cardio-pulmonary resuscitation) to people in need of it. This is a skill that is needful when someone's life is in danger of being lost due to their inability to breathe, or in the event their heart is failing, or has ceased to function. In such an instance, it could be said that death is attempting to leave samples. I'm sure no sane person would allow death to leave samples of his product at their door if they knew who was knocking.

Sadly, there is one of the key issues. Too many people, even Christians, do not realize that many of the things they sample daily in life are nothing but samples left by death in hopes that passers-by at that point in life would sample them, not knowing what it is of which they are partaking. But if one knows divine CPR, the art of guarding one's heart at all times, and continually feeding the heart with the Word of God, not only are such samples recognized, but they can be removed or destroyed by the Christian who knows how to administer holy CPR.

John 10:10

The thief cometh not,
but for to steal,
and to kill,
and to destroy:
I am come that they might have life,
and that they might have it more abundantly.

Ephesians 5:11-12

And have no fellowship
with the unfruitful works of darkness,
but rather reprove them.
For it is a shame even to speak of those things
which are done of them in secret.

Psalm 27:14

Wait on the LORD:
be of good courage,
and he shall strengthen thine heart:
wait, I say, on the LORD.

In today's world, being certified in first aid care is required of many people in various professional arenas outside the medical field. Law enforcement, fire fighters, educators, and more require regular and ongoing training. CPR (cardio-pulmonary resuscitation) is often a part of those requirements. While I am by no means an authority on first aid and CPR, I have had training in those arenas, and understand CPR as working to restore, or resuscitate necessary heart, or pulmonary function, to sustain life. It may involve chest compressions, rescue breathing (resuscitation), and in advanced cases, possibly the use of a defibrillator, a device used to stimulate, or *jump-start* the heart into a proper rhythm to sustain life. Having been trained to some degree, having seen this work done by professionals in stressful situations, and knowing people who live productive lives due to the proper use of CPR, I am amazed by what mankind has learned about the human body. It is truly fascinating.

And natural CPR is not limited to the arena of first aid. Even during a surgical procedure, a cardio-thoracic surgeon may use electrical stimulation, or even used his own hands to help stimulate the heart muscle. Once again, it is truly amazing.

In daily life, I have observed that many more people need spiritual CPR than require natural CPR. I have likewise concluded that if proper spiritual health practices as it regards the human spirit were observed, far less spiritual CPR would be necessary. Sadly, I have likewise noted in life that there seems to be far fewer people qualified to administer spiritual CPR than are needed in this hour. That, dear reader, needs to change. Let us pray that our Lord would raise up and prepare truly able ministers of the New Covenant who are supernaturally endued with the desperately needed skill of administering spiritual CPR.

While this writing is not intended to be an exhaustive study on this topic, I do wish to address the matter with enough insight to provide launch points for anyone desiring to engage in true spiritual CPR.

Cardiac Compressions

In the natural realm, cardiac compressions are controlled thrusts on the sternum of a person whose heart has stopped. In the realm of the spirit, it is the application of a controlled touch, or impact, on the spirit of someone who needs to be revived. For as long as I can remember, churches have held revivals. In that term alone is a volume of discussion on how words we use in the church have taken on a life of their own. To *revive* is to return to consciousness or restore to life. Think about that. The implication is that one has been, at some point in the past, conscious and alive, has ceased to exist in that state, or at least drastically pulled back from the state, and has once again had normal heart function restored.

(Allow me to briefly allude to an admonition for giving honor before continuing on. 1 Timothy 5:17 clearly states that elders who labor in "word and doctrine" should be accounted worthy of "double honor." Then in James 3:1, we read that "masters," or what we might today call leaders will receive a "greater condemnation" in judgment. When those two passages are placed side-by-side, a sobering picture is painted. To that end, while I write for anyone who would desire to read truth, I pray that men and women in leadership in the body of Christ, and especially those who are placed in offices of the five-fold ministry by the Lord Jesus, would pay special attention here.)

If anyone in the natural world should hold the deepest understanding and skill in administering CPR, it should be those who are formally trained in medical procedures, especially those who are recognized as true medical doctors. By the same token, if there are people in the earth who hold deep understanding of spiritual CPR, it should be those who are leaders in the body of Christ, and especially those in the five-fold ministry. And of that final group, if any of the five-fold ministry possesses such understanding, it should be *pastors*. Having pastored one church for 28 years, I can speak to that matter from an experiential standpoint. I recall a moment early in my pastoral ministry when the Lord spoke to my heart and said, "Keep your ear to My heart and your hand on the pulse of the church. Keep them together, for in that is the life of your pastoral work." So, once again I speak to those in the five-fold ministry. You *will* be called upon, and that likely frequently, to administer spiritual CPR. Stay ready and alert.

Allow me a few questions. I am writing about touching, and even impacting the heart of God's people. Always remember that it is the responsibility of the believer to reach the lost with the message of Christ. But for that to take place in a powerful and large-scale manner, the Church, the light of the world, and the salt of the earth, needs to be fully awake in Christ. In other words, the Church *must* be revived; returned to a state of full consciousness and fully restored life. And for the Church, that means a lot of spiritual CPR. So, here are the questions. What are you doing to touch the heart of the people to whom you minister in the body of Christ? What are you doing to impact them? What are you saying? How are you going about applying spiritual CPR to those whose spirit needs to be strengthened for the work at hand? I believe these questions can be answered with a few basic truths set forth in the Word of God.

Child of God, begin with the Word. Hear the Scriptures. Read what Jehovah would say about it.

- **2 Timothy 2:15** – "Study to shew thyself approved unto God, a workman that needeth not to be ashamed, rightly dividing the word of truth."
- **Joshua 1:8** – "This book of the law shall not depart out of thy mouth; but thou shalt meditate therein day and night, that thou mayest observe to do according to all that is written therein: for then thou shalt make thy way prosperous, and then thou shalt have good success."
- **Proverbs 4:20-23** – "My son, attend to my words; incline thine ear unto my sayings. Let them not depart from thine eyes; keep them in the midst of thine heart. For they *are* life unto those that find them, and health to all their flesh. Keep thy heart with all diligence; for out of it *are* the issues of life."
- **Psalm 107:20** – "He sent His Word and healed them, and delivered them from their destructions."
- **Isaiah 53:5** – "But he *was* wounded for our transgressions, *he* was bruised for our iniquities: the chastisement of our peace *was* upon him; and with his stripes we are healed."
- **Matthew 8:17** – "That it might be fulfilled which was spoken by Esaias the prophet, saying, Himself took our infirmities, and bare *our* sicknesses."
- **1 Peter 2:24** – "Who his own self bare our sins in his own body on the tree, that we, being dead to sins, should live unto righteousness: by whose stripes ye were healed."

While this is by no means an exhaustive representation of what the Scriptures have to say about healing, it does lay a strong foundation upon which to build. Since faith comes by hearing and hearing by the Word of God (Romans 10;17), and since faith is a product of the heart (spirit), every indication points to the application of the Word of God as a major element of pulmonary compression. The Word of God, being heard, has a direct impact on the spirit-man. It does, in fact, place a certain pressure on the human spirit to believe, for it is indeed truth. And such should be a regularly applied treatment to the human spirit at every opportunity the man or woman of God has to speak.

The fact that the Word that is preached needs to be "rightly" divided (2 Timothy 2:15) gives clear indication that it is not to be recklessly applied, but it should be done with extreme accuracy, and under the direct supervision of the Head of staff, the Lord Jesus Himself via Holy Spirit. And if the Word can be *rightly* divided, then it could also be *wrongly* divided. The one administering spiritual CPR carries grave responsibility in that work. Just a thought.

Another element of Holy CPR is the parallel of rescue breathing. In rescue breathing, the goal is to help supply oxygen to the body during the pulmonary compressions. At one time, it was accomplished via mouth-to-mouth resuscitation. According to EMT's (emergency medical technicians) working at this writing, it is not considered nearly as important as the pulmonary compressions, but may still be done, now utilizing certain devices designed for that purpose. Still, the desired result is the same – supply necessary oxygen to someone who is not breathing on his/her own. So, how would this apply to the spiritual realm?

There are so many people (including many Christians) who live in a spiritual atmosphere that is so polluted they are spiritually suffocating. They are in desperate need of the fresh breath of the Lord breathing into their life. Think about the breath of God for a moment. God breathed life into the nostrils of Adam in the garden of Eden. It was a great wind that arose that divided the Red Sea for the children of Israel to cross. It was a rushing, mighty wind that filled the house on the day of Pentecost. Each of these are representations of a spiritual atmosphere in which the breath of God is evident, and in which a believer can thrive. And of course, let us not forget the moment in which Jesus breathed on His disciples and told them to receive the Holy Spirit (John 20:22).

Thinking on and examining these events, let us ask ourselves what we are doing in our daily lives to breathe life into the people we encounter? How are we serving to create an atmosphere in which the life of God can freely flow and be manifest? What life are we living? What examples are we being? What words are we speaking? What example are we setting?

And concerning the potential third element of CPR, the use of a defibrillator, what would our role be in the realm of the spirit? In the natural, this is the use of a device that causes the flow of electrical current to the heart in an attempt to either re-start it, or to establish a normal cardiac rhythm. But how does this work in the realm of the Spirit?

I believe it is seen in those encounters with people whose walk with Christ has ceased, or whose walk with Him is, at best, sporadic, lacking consistency. At those times, what do we carry in our lives that would make it possible to jump-start, or re-start their walk with the Lord, or if need be, to help that person snap back by awakening them to their need for daily communion with their Lord and Savior?

First, I believe, is the anointing you have received from the Lord as a child of God and joint heir with Christ. That anointing will differ in different people, but there is still an anointing in you that has been placed there by the Lord that is the launching point for a divinely appointed function and service as a member of the body of Christ. It is that anointing that you have within you (or anointings) upon which Holy Spirit comes to manifest His power through your life to the world. 1 John 2 declares that the anointing you have received of the Lord teaches you, thus preparing you to always be ready to comply with the leading of Holy Spirit, thereby allowing the flow of His power through your life.

With that anointing, you may be called upon by Holy Spirit to speak a word in due season, a word fitly framed at an appropriate time for a divinely appointed purpose. And with that spoken word, possibly an action of some sort; laying hands on someone, passing an anointed handkerchief to someone, or giving something you possess to someone in need. When these things are done in compliance with Holy Spirit as you walk in your anointing, moments of *divine charisma;* that personal insertion by God of His presence for purposes of power that rise above all that is humanly possible, occur. In short, *supernatural!*

Once again, I must declare this writing is in no way intended to be exhaustive in its content. Rather, it is intended to inspire, motivate, and urgently encourage the reader to allow Holy Spirit to prepare him for the desperately needed application of spiritual CPR when the wounded, failing, and desperate are found.

CHAPTER ELEVEN

Only Candidates Get Elected
(Heir – Candidate – Elect)

Imagine living a life in which your body is bowed over, bent over at the waist, and existing in that condition for 18 years. Imagine not being able to look directly into the faces of the people around you, or even your own spouse or grown children. Imagine living all those years without the ability to look up and see the sky by day or the stars by night. Imagine the discomfort that comes from living every mobile moment of your life for 18 years bowed over at the waist. Imagine the thoughts that created a flash flood of emotion when she hears the voice of life say, "Woman, thou are loosed from thine infirmity." Imagine the volcanic eruption of joy when the man whose voice she heard touched her, and she was immediately made straight. Imagine!

Every work Jesus did carried significance. In that significance is a lesson to learn. Why did this woman, the seed of Abraham, not know the things she heard Jesus say? Why did she have to live as she had for 18 years? The answer should be obvious. She did not know her covenant. She did not know she was an heir, a candidate, and the elect of God by an overwhelming and unanimous vote of ***ONE****.*

(Luke 13:10-17)

Isaiah 42:1

Behold my servant, whom I uphold;
mine elect, in whom my soul delighteth;
I have put my spirit upon him:
he shall bring forth judgment to the Gentiles.

Isaiah 65:22-23

They shall not build, and another inhabit;
they shall not plant, and another eat:
for as the days of a tree are the days of my people,
and mine elect shall long enjoy the work of their hands.
They shall not labour in vain, nor bring forth for trouble;
for they are the seed of the blessed of the LORD,
and their offspring with them.

Peter 1:2

Elect according to the foreknowledge of God the Father,
through sanctification of the Spirit,
unto obedience and sprinkling of the blood of Jesus Christ:
Grace unto you, and peace, be multiplied.

Romans 8:31-33

What shall we then say to these things?
If God be for us, who can be against us?
He that spared not his own Son,
but delivered him up for us all,
how shall he not with him also freely give us all things?
Who shall lay any thing to the charge of God's elect?
It is God that justifieth.

In the political world, governors and presidents in the United States are elected. But being elected does not place them in office immediately. From the moment of their election until the time he/she takes office, the elected individual is referred to as governor-elect, or president-elect. Though elected, they have yet to be inaugurated. And it is only after their inauguration that official-elect officially enters the office to which he/she has been elected.

During that interim between election and inauguration, it is generally accepted that the official elect will be actively engaged in doing all he can to be as prepared as possible to enter the office to which he has been elected.

On July 6, 1986 I entered what would become a 28-year pastorate. I stepped out of that office on July 6, 2014. In January, 2010, the Lord revealed to me a number of things; (1) the departure date for me from that pastorate; (2) who would be my replacement in that ministry office; (3) how I was to handle the transition. I informed my board at our February meeting of the agenda, but did not name my replacement. That had to be revealed first to the young man who would become pastor of the church, and it had to come from the Lord. In March, 2010, I shared the same information with my leadership team. Finally, in October, 2010, the young man in question set a luncheon appointment with me, and upon our meeting, said to me, "Pastor, I believe I'm the man for the job." I agreed immediately, and asked him what took so long? It had been given him by the Lord, for no one other than two close and trusted prayer partners and I knew his name, and even to them, it was the Lord Who had revealed it, not me.

In the church's annual business meeting in January, 2011, I presented him to our congregation, and he was unanimously ratified as "pastor-elect" of our church. Over the following three and one-half years, I did all I could to train, teach, prepare, partner with, inform, and raise him up for the task before him, and at this point in time (2021), he is doing a great job. We could say he was elected before he was inaugurated.

Now let us turn that thinking to our walk with the Lord. Please take time to consider what I write. Examine the truth of the statements I make in light of God's Word, and not on traditional statements most Christians have heard at some time. For a moment, let's turn our attention to what it means to be one of God's "elect." It is really a simple concept. When one is elected in the political process at any level, it is generally the person who receives the most votes who get elected. They are said to have received the popular vote, or the majority of the voting population. In the Greek language of the New Testament, to be "elect" declares a person to be the selected person. In this case, the selection was by God. It speaks of the "elect" as a favorite person. In this case, the "elect" is indeed God's favorite, or one who has received His grace. And finally, to be the "elect" of God declares such a person to be chosen specifically by God. That makes it a very personal and individual thing that has taken place.

So, if you are one of those people, one of God's "elect," one of those He has Personally selected, looked upon by Him as His favorite, and specifically chosen by Him, you are among a very special race of beings called "new creatures in Christ" (2 Corinthians 5:17-21). You are among a new species that never existed before the resurrection of Jesus from the dead. You are a new creation in Christ Jesus!

As a human being, you have been listed as an heir of God since before the foundation of the world. Shocked? Don't be. Consider the Word. The Scriptures declare that Jesus was crucified before the foundation of the world. Why was Jesus crucified? Read John 3:16, and Luke 4:18-19. He was crucified so the lost could be saved, the sick could be healed, the bound could be delivered, and the poor could live in abundance.

And let us move forward with this thought. Where in the Scriptures does it say that one's name is written in the book of life when you get saved? That, dear reader, is not in the Word of God. Before anyone could be born again, which was *after* the resurrection of Jesus, He spoke to His disciples in Luke 10 and told them to rejoice because their names were "written in heaven." When He told this wonderful news, no one had ever been born again. So, when were their names written in heaven? They were surely written there when the plan of redemption was established and the "whosoever" rule was set in place, that being before the foundation of the world. So that you may see for yourself the basis for these statements, I offer you the following Scripture references. Matthew 25:34; Ephesians 1:4; Ephesians 4:3; 1 Peter 1:20.

And I further encourage you to read the following passages concerning the "book of life" and that which is written in it. Revelation 3:5; Revelation 13:7-8; Revelation 20:12-15; Revelation 22:19. Concerning the things written in the book of life, I find it interesting that at no point does it state that any additional names would be written in it, but the Scriptures do, and emphatically so, state that there would be cause for names to be "blotted out" of the book of life.

Based on these Scriptures, I propose to you that God so loved the world from before the foundation of the world, that before mankind ever existed in the flesh, by His great love and foreknowledge, your name and mine was already written in the book of life, for Father's intention was that none should perish, but that all should come to the repentance (2 Peter 3:9). Based on that truth, I can boldly declare to you that from before the foundation of the world, God intended you to be His heir. You see, it was not the act of a democracy or a republic, nor by a simple majority vote of many or few. Rather, it was by the action of our omnipotent and sovereign God that your name was written there, and in being written there, you have been set forth as an heir-elect.

Then the day you were conceived in your mother's womb, the God who knew you there, once again by His Own sovereign vote, declared you to be a candidate for the eternal life in Christ. At some point in time, when you had your first opportunity to receive by your own choice, Jesus as Lord, but refused, you made a spiritual declaration that you were no longer a candidate. But God, Whose Word is settled forever in heaven, denied your refusal, and because He loves you so much, continue to keep you in the race.

Then on that day, at that moment when you confessed Jesus as your Lord, believing in your heart that God had raised Him from the dead, not only was your candidacy reaffirmed, but you now became an elected official in the kingdom of God. But once again, keep in mind that your election was not one of a popular vote by the masses, but rather an election by One; our great Sovereign, Jehovah God. He put your name on His list as a candidate to receive the life of God in you. Even when you ran from the responsibility that would be yours to truly live, He kept you as a candidate. When such a person leaves this life without having accepted the role of being one of the elect, that name is blotted out of the book of life. But if you DO accept that role, you are one of His elect.

And to such a person, to that individual that believes on Him, to that person, to that elect individual, God gives the power to become a son of God (John 1:12-14). This "power to become a son of God" is both the privilege and responsibility of every believer in Christ, and once born again, should be utilized to grow up into Christ unto the perfect man (Ephesians 4:11-16). Once again, it is not only a wonderful and divinely-given supernatural privilege, but it is also a powerful and divinely-designated responsibility. My reader friend, accept it. And here is a major part of the reason why. As an heir of God and a joint-heir with Christ, you are the seed of Abraham and an heir according to the promise (Galatians 3:29).

From before the foundation of the world you were designated to be an heir of God and a joint-heir with Christ, your name being written in the book of life. When you were conceived in your mother's womb, you were designated by the only vote that counts in eternity as a candidate to receive eternal life. The moment you were born again, you became one of God's elect, one of His children, and were given the power to become a "son" of God. And that is the very thing that nature itself cries out to see – the manifestation of the sons of God (Romans 8:19).

But what does all this have to do with the focus of this book, the Covenant of Health? And the answer is, much, and in every way. Healing is part of the covenant, as it is a part of salvation. When the word "salvation" is examined in the fullness of its intended meaning, healing is a vital part of that meaning. Follow the steps from the previous paragraph to see the fit of healing within the New Covenant. From the foundation of the world, when you were designated to be an heir of God and joint-heir with Christ, you were designated to be healed, and more, to be healthy. From the moment of your conception in your mother's womb, you were made a candidate, eligible to receive healing and health as it is set forth in the New Covenant. The moment you were born again and became one of God's elect, you were made an elect for healing and health as set forth in the New Covenant for all children of God (Isaiah 53:4-5; 1 Peter 2:24). And as you grow in the Spirit from being a spiritual infant to becoming a mature, equipped, and well-enabled son of God, you should become deeply knowledgeable of your covenant privilege and responsibility to live healed and healthy (3 John 2-4).

In all of these scenarios and examples, one element should be clearly obvious to us. Healing and health are the absolute will of God for His people, and the process by which you can walk in the healing and health element of the New Covenant began before the foundation of the world. With something so obvious, having such a long and literally eternal heritage, why would anyone, especially the believer, not take the necessary steps in life to walk in the full blessing of that covenant?

Now one additional point needs to be made in this chapter. Jesus called healing "the children's bread" (Matthew 15:26; Mark 7:27). If healing is "the children's bread," then the mention of healing according to the Scriptures, the administration of healing by whatever Biblical means are applied, the resulting work of healing in the person receiving ministry, and the walk of health in a covenant child of God should sound forth like the ringing of a dinner bell. With that in mind, think of this. When the dinner bell was rung for the people to come eat, the animals that belonged to them would have learned that it was feeding time. Do you remember the story of the Syrophoenician woman who came to Jesus for her daughter's healing? Jesus told her it would not be proper for Him to take "the children's bread" and give it to the dogs. His use of the term "dogs" was a reference to those not living in covenant with the Lord; in this case, the gentiles.

But what was her response to Jesus? She said, "Even the dogs get the crumbs." Jesus responded to her, "For this saying, go your way. Your daughter is whole." Think of that. Even the crumbs that fall from "the children's bread" are powerful enough to bring healing to a sinner; to the lost. Do you see it? The plan of God was that healing and health be a part of one's normal existence. One of the great purposes of Jesus on the cross was to make that healing and health available to every human being, and that without reservation. To that end I urge every child of God to ring the dinner bell. Let the whole world know that Jesus has provided healing and health for "whosoever will." And if you're a "whosoever," you're included.

CHAPTER TWELVE

Soul Prosperity

The Lord Jesus said He would give to us the keys of the kingdom. One of the greatest keys one can possess as it relates to the kingdom of God is the key to soul prosperity.

It is clearly revealed to us in the Scriptures. It is easy to understand in its revelation. And yet it seems to be utilized so little in the day-to-day living of God's people. Why?

In life, it seems that almost everyone has a will to win. Sadly, however, it is but a few of those who have the will to win who also possess the will to prepare to win. Those are the ones who pay the price. No normal person wants to lose, but the price to pay through the will to prepare to win is not cheap. It is high. So is the price one must pay to walk in soul prosperity, for to attain to soul prosperity there must exist a strong will to prepare to win. Therein is the rub. Do you possess the will to prepare to win? You have opposition, but through faith, the total victory can be yours.

Psalm 23:3

He restoreth my soul:

Psalm 103:1

A Psalm of David. Bless the LORD, O my soul: and all that is within me, bless his holy name.

Jonah 2:7

When my soul fainted within me I remembered the LORD: and my prayer came in unto thee, into thine holy temple.

Mark 8:36

For what shall it profit a man, if he shall gain the whole world, and lose his own soul?

John 12:27

Now is my soul troubled; and what shall I say? Father, save me from this hour: but for this cause came I unto this hour.

Romans 12:2

And be not conformed to this world: but be ye transformed by the renewing of your mind, that ye may prove what is that good, and acceptable, and perfect, will of God.

3 John 2

Beloved, I wish above all things that thou mayest prosper and be in health, even as thy soul prospereth.

Soul prosperity. Now there is a term that, sadly, does not appear to be as familiar to the body of Christ as it should be. Let this writer be clear. A clear understanding of soul prosperity is more essential than ever to living a life of divine healing, and ultimately, divine health. Divine healing is a common term in Christian circles, regardless of one's position on the deeper topic. It is really simple. It means healing that comes from a divine source, meaning the Lord. It really is that simple. Healing that comes to us by way of the Lord is divine healing. It can come as a gift of the Spirit, one of the gifts of healings, by the laying on of hands, by using anointing oil, through taking Communion, by one's personal faith in God and the Word, and other ways the Lord may institute. One thing we should never do is limit the Lord in what He desires to do.

Then there is the term, divine health. While we don't often hear that term, it is a cut above divine healing. You see, when one is in health, one does not need divine healing. Jesus certainly lived in divine health. There was no sickness nor disease that could take hold in His life while on this earth. The only time sickness or disease touched Him was when He went to Calvary for us, for in that journey, He was "wounded for our transgressions, *He was* bruised for our iniquities: the chastisement of our peace was upon Him; and with His stripes we are healed" (Isaiah 53:5). Since then, there have been others who have walked in that level of covenant. For example, we see it in the immunity of Apostle Paul to a venomous snake bite. Others like John G. Lake walked in it for at least a portion of their earthly lives. It is still available to every believer, but it is a level of covenant most folks have not been willing to pay the price to attain, and there is a price. Yes, Jesus has paid the full price for our redemption, and in that redemption is our healing. But to live a life that is above any attempt of sickness and disease to affect you requires a commitment to the Word of God and time in the Word of God until the covenant is so firmly established in your mind (soul), that absolutely nothing can cause it to waiver in the slightest. Such a lifestyle does not arise naturally, but requires the work of the supernatural to be daily manifest in your life. And once again, let it be firmly established, for such, there is a cost.

When one considers the term soul prosperity, perhaps the best passage of Scripture to examine is found in 3 John 2. There we read, "Beloved, I wish above all things that thou mayest prosper and be in health, even as thy soul prospereth." Let us consider that passage the point from which to launch this examination.

The book of Third John was written to Gaius, a Christian believer and brother in Christ to John the Apostle. And since we know that all Scripture is given by the inspiration of God for the church, we can receive the words of 3 John as having been written to the Church. And if we accept it as being written to the Church, we can accept it as being written to the individual believer. Therefore, the first word of the second verse, "Beloved," is speaking directly to you.

The next portion of this verse is powerful beyond description. "I wish above all things…." (3 John 2). Stop for a moment and think on that phrase. God states His personal desire for His beloved. When one wishes above all things, the clear indication is that there can be no higher desire. In other words, God is saying that He is about to reveal His highest personal desire and pleasure for His beloved. He desires *nothing* more highly for His beloved than this….

"....that thou mayest prosper and be in health...." (3 John 2). Think of that. God's highest desire, God's greatest pleasure for His people, His "beloved," is that they "prosper and be in health." It could not be more clearly stated. This is the Word of God. This is the Word that Father has exalted above His Name. This is the Word of His power by which He is upholding all things. This *is* the undeniable Word and will of God for His people.

If the Word cited here had ended with those words, it would surely have been enough to establish His will, and just as surely given us a target at which we should aim and a goal toward which we should strive for complete attainment. *But....but....but,* the stated Word of the Lord in 3 John 2 did *not* stop there. He took the next step to reveal to us the means by which such a lofty holy desire could be attained. Let's read the entire verse, uninterrupted by discussion. "Beloved, I wish above all things that thou mayest prosper and be in health, even as thy soul prospereth."

There! Did you see it? The answer to the question of *how* one attains to *soul prosperity*. Look at 3 John 2 again.

- "Beloved" – that's you and me; His children
- "I wish" – that's Father's desire
- "above all things" – there is no desire above this for His children
- "that thou mayest prosper" – it says what it says. Father does *not* want His people poor or living in need
- "and be in health" – once again, it says what it says. This is better than healing. This is living in divine health; health that is provided through divine covenant with our divine God.

- "even as thy soul prospereth." – the soul (mind, will, intellect, and emotion). Remember, you *are* a spirit, you *have* a soul, and you *live in* a body. The spirit is that part of man which is born again. The soul is that part of man that reasons and through its acceptance of God's reasoning, can enjoy the benefits of salvation. And your body is the earthly suit in which you live; the temple of Holy Ghost.

So, here it is clearly revealed. The secret, if indeed it is a secret, to living in divine health is *soul prosperity*. The question then arises, just what is *soul prosperity*? Let us now lend ourselves to that discovery. And it begins with clearly recognizing what the soul is. The word from which soul arises in the Greek language is *psuche*, from which words such as psychology also have their origin. We need to understand that the spirit and soul are *not* the same thing. The human spirit is who one really is. You *are* a spirit. The body is the clothing of the human spirit, or to use a Biblical term, the body is the temple. It is that mechanism that allows the spirit and soul to have an outlet for their creativity, desire, and emotions. It is the device used by the spirit and soul for their expression. The soul is that element of the human being that is comprised of the mind (the processor), will (the determiner), intellect (intelligence), and emotions (what we call feelings.) With that in mind, let us examine the elements we must consider in causing the soul to prosper.

Soul Prosperity – the Mind

The Scripture is very plain in its wording, especially in Romans 12:2. There we read, "And be not conformed to this world: but be ye transformed by the renewing of your mind, that ye may prove what *is* that good, and acceptable, and perfect, will of God." We are told in Philippians 2:5 to "let this mind be in you which was also in Christ Jesus." The "mind" is that part of the soul that entertains opinion or sentiment. We could say that it is the thinking part of the soul. Would it not seem to be reasonable to state that the highest possible manifestation of soul prosperity as it relates to the mind would be to have the mind of Christ? That would indicate that one is entertaining the sentiments and opinions of Christ, and surely, there are no sentiments or opinions higher than His. Consider Apostle Paul's instruction to the Philippians in chapter 4, verse 8; "Finally, brethren, whatsoever things *are* true, whatsoever things *are* honest, whatsoever things *are* just, whatsoever things *are* pure, whatsoever things *are* lovely, whatsoever things *are* of good report; if *there be* any virtue, and if *there be* any praise, think on these things." Here, plainly stated, are the opinions and sentiments that comprise the mind of Christ, and as such, should be the pattern of use for the Christian mind. Herein is found mind prosperity. And to maintain that supernatural mind-prosperity, the ongoing, day-to-day, never-ending work of renewing the mind needs to be done. Take a moment and read the Romans 12:2 passage. See it clearly. You are "transformed" by the "renewing of your mind." The *ing* ending on the word "renewing" is a gerund, and in this case means an ongoing process, not a one-time action.

Soul Prosperity – the Will

A person's *will* identifies one's personal choice, desire, preference, or wish. Consider one of the most poignant moments in Scripture. Jesus was praying in the Garden of Gethsemane. As He prayed, He said to the Father, "Abba, Father, all things *are* possible unto thee; take away this cup from me: nevertheless not what I will, but what thou wilt" (Mark 16:36). From much earlier in His life, He was aware of the price He would be called upon to pay for the redemption of man. He was keenly aware of the suffering that would ensue, of the torment He must bear, of the mocking, derision, scourging, abuse, and cursing that would be cast upon Him, not to mention the crucifixion itself. From His Own words we see clearly that it was *not* His will to endure all this. It was not His personal choice, His desire, His preference, or His wish. But though it was *not* His will, He, by the act of obedience in faith, set His own will aside, yielding fully to the plan He had made with Father before the foundation of the world.

One can rest assured that Jesus *never* did anything that in any way violated the will of His Father. Simply stated, He fully yielded His will to the will of Father, regardless of how Father's will impacted Him. He *fully* submitted to the will of Father, regardless of cost. And when we speak of soul prosperity in relation to one's will, this is the perfect example of manifested soul prosperity.

Therefore, soul prosperity for the believer today, as it relates to will, would best be described as imitation of our Lord's action in this arena that we willfully, and with unyielding determination, bring our will into full compliance with that of Father. And that, my friend, requires a dynamic work of faith on the believer's part. Such faith requires the continual application of the Word of God in compliance with Romans 10:17, and the will to carry that out will be greatly dependent upon the active work of Galatians 5:6. When these two Scriptures function together as the Lord intended, foundation for all needed support to one's will is sure. And once again I tell you, as with the renewing of the mind, this is not a one-step process, but a daily, life-long process to which one must give one's self to continually keep one's will fully submitted to the will of Father.

Soul Prosperity – the Intellect

I have often been asked how intellect relates to one's soul, or the psuche realm of the human being. Like the mind, will, and emotions, the intellect is a directly connected element of the soul. I believe that in most cases, when one thinks of intellect, one thinks of intelligence, some level of education, or that which is related to one's academic life. But just like mind and will, *everything* that enters through the sense gates (sight, hearing, touch, taste, smell) is, at the very least, examined to some degree by one's intellect. Intellect has a strong role to play in directing one to leave a burning building, in determining what one considers humorous or threatening, and reaching conclusions about what one considers useful for living. I suppose you could say that one's intellect is composed of the collective data one has received through the sense gates and can be utilized in the work of reasoning and decision-making.

Have you ever burned yourself accidentally? Have you ever struck your thumb with a hammer? Have you ever been physically assaulted and experienced pain from that assault? To each of them you reacted or responded. Do you know how to read and write? Can you accurately perform basic math functions? Can you communicate in a reasonable fashion? While all these have likely brought both thoughtful and willful responses, each is directly attached to one's intellect. Each of these elements and actions represent intellectual function.

Now consider this. While I would leave the mathematical calculations to an Einstein, I would not necessarily trust him to fly a plane in which I was a passenger, nor would I trust him to perform spinal surgery on my body. Why? The answer is simple. When one utilizes his intellect, it becomes obvious where his education, training, and strengths lie. It is what we study and apply *in* our lives that largely determines the flow *through* our intellect *out* of our lives. So, when we speak of the renewing of one's psuche realm, the question arises, "What are you consuming intellectually?"

Your intellectual consumption will largely determine your intellectual production. In computer terminology, we have the acrostic GIGO – garbage in – garbage out. The same principle can be applied to one's intellect. Are you feeding your intellect high grade information? Useful data? Health and healing? Understanding of business? Television news? Gossip? Garbage? Once again, your intellectual consumption will largely determine your intellectual production. Feed your intellect well, just as a top athlete would feed his body well. And like a top athlete who trains his body well, so train your intellect to function at its highest potential.

Soul Prosperity – the Emotions

Human emotions are human emissions. Keeping that statement in mind, here are a few questions for your consideration. Do we expect industry to control the emissions of their industry? Do we expect our automobiles to run as cleanly and efficiently as possible? Do we (in truly civilized society) treat raw sewage in some manner before disposing of it? And the answer to these and similar questions is "Yes." All these are issues of emissions that come out of society at some level.

Why then can we not realize that our emotions need similar actions applied to them. This is one of the arenas in which the words of Jesus are so poignant. He said, "The children of this world are wiser in their generation than the children of light" (Luke 16:9). The world has enough sense to work to make their emissions safe, but so many in the church give *no* effort to controlling their emotions, and by failing to do so, often pollute the work of the church to the point of making it as corrupt as the world, and even sickening the population of the church. It's time to awake, my friend, and clean up our act. We need to renew our emotional filter system, keep it clean by the washing of the water of the Word, prevent ourselves from flawed thinking, and govern ourselves to keep safe emotional systems in place in our daily living.

Soul prosperity is no laughing matter to the church. It is *not* to be pushed aside as some new doctrine that the traditional church may frown upon or for which it may show some disdain. Yes, there are those who have taken it, like so many other sound elements of our faith, to the extreme. But just because someone has taken it upon themselves to produce counterfeit money does not mean that all other humans should discard their money and not use it for a legitimate and beneficial purpose. Think of it in this manner. There can be no counterfeit unless there is a real, legitimate, purposeful, and needful element worthy of counterfeiting. The enemy of your soul works tirelessly to produce counterfeits to deceive and destroy the church. Should we, the church, not be even more tireless in our efforts to learn, teach, disciple, model, and deploy the truths of God's kingdom that the enemy is attempting to counterfeit?

Our work is before us. Surely soul prosperity is one of the strong keys given to us by the Lord to unlock the treasures of heaven in our lives in limitless manner. Let us rise to the occasion, and be not conformed to this world, but be transformed by the renewing of our mind, will, intellect, and emotions so we may prove what is that good and acceptable and perfect will of Father. That is our assignment. Let us enter into the field of this labor that we might ultimately leave that field bringing a great harvest with us.

CHAPTER THIRTEEN

All the Father Wants You to Know

Our Heavenly Father does not desire His people to be in any way ignorant. That statement is undeniably true, especially when examined in the light of what the Scriptures have to say about Father's intended relationship with us, His desire for us, His work in us, and the manifestation of His power through us. Open yourself fully to all Father has for you. Most Christians are living pathetically short of Father's intentions for their lives. Be one of this generation to change that. You can choose to be one of those agents right now. It's work . . . hard work. Are you willing to apply yourself to it? If you are, I offer you the following thoughts so that, prayerfully, you will take up the mantle that has fallen before you.

When Elisha took up the mantle of Elijah, and coming to the Jordan River, he asked, "Where is the Lord God of Elijah?" (2 Kings 2:14) My question today turns on that question. Today I ask you, "Where are the Elisha's of the Lord God?"

John 16:13-15

Howbeit when he,
the Spirit of truth, is come,
he will guide you into all truth:
for he shall not speak of himself;
but whatsoever he shall hear,
that shall he speak:
and he will shew you things to come.

He shall glorify me:
for he shall receive of mine,
and shall shew it unto you.

All things that the Father hath are mine:
therefore said I, that he shall take of mine,
and shall shew it unto you.

1 Corinthians 2:16

For who hath known the mind of the Lord,
that he may instruct him?
But we have the mind of Christ.

The purpose of this writing is in no way intended to say to you all the Father wants you to know. There is not enough space in this, or for that matter, a multitude of books, to cover that topic, even superficially. That is a work that requires nothing less than the personal hand of deity through the work of Holy Spirit.

The purpose of this writing is to address specifically one of the great covenant issues extended to us in our redemption – *healing* – and further, both *divine healing* and *divine health*, to which I believe there are *four* basic foundational pillars upon which one can rest in full assurance that healing and health belongs to every covenant child of God, and it belongs to them in the fullest.

To begin our discussion, let's examine John 16:13-15. Take a close look at what the Lord Jesus tells us in those verses. Look at what belongs to you, as a believer; as a Christian; as a child of God. On the day of Pentecost, Holy Spirit came for a specific work to and for the church. While this passage is certainly not exhaustive in His work for, to, and through us, it does indeed set forth a foundation for our discussion here.

In the passage in question, when Holy Ghost came on the day of Pentecost, He came to . . .

- guide us into all truth
- speak whatsoever He heard, not of Himself
- show you (the believer) things to come
- glorify Jesus
- receive of that which belongs to Jesus and show it to you (the believer)

Then Jesus added the following statement. He said, "All things that the Father hath are Mine: therefore said I, that He shall take of Mine, and shall show it unto you" (John 16:15). What a powerful statement this is by Jesus, and that statement is to *you*! It can be made no clearer. Our Lord wants you to *know* who you are, *know* what He has given you, and to *know* how to go about walking in the fullness of his blessing. In this writing, I focus on the issues of *divine healing and divine health*. In particular I want to focus on what I call the *Four Pillars of Divine Healing and Divine Health.*

Consider how one goes about building a structure that needs to endure. It requires a firm foundation, solid footing, and a form that can withstand a scrutinizing measurement of success. God has firmly and clearly established such a foundation, footing, and form as it regards divine healing and divine health. I am convinced that what I am about to share with you is based surely on the foundation He established concerning a divine covenant of health that He has set forth for all who would call on the Name of the Lord.

...PILLAR NUMBER ONE...

Demonstration of Ability

I do not personally know any true Christian that does not believe God has the *ability* to heal. That great truth has been demonstrated from the beginning. Time and again in the Old Testament (King Hezekiah, Naaman the Syrian, children at the hand of Elijah and Elisha, the children of Israel in Egypt, the children of Israel in the wilderness, and many more) we have seen His ability. Throughout the Gospels (by the hands, words, and works of Jesus, as well as

His charge to His disciples) it was clearly demonstrated. It is no less demonstrated in the New Testament at the hands of believers. And then from the close of the book of Acts even until today, the ability of God to heal has been continually demonstrated. I can boldly attest to more healings at the hand of God than I can innumerate in this writing, many of which have happened within my own body. I am the personal recipient of the healing power of God from broken bones, neuropathy, diabetes, malaria, and more. I have witnessed it for my bride, our children, our parents, and our grandchildren in our family. I have witnessed it for my friends and family in Christ in multitudinous fashion, and have heard their testimonies. And I have witnessed it for multitudes of people I do not know, but was made aware of the circumstances they faced and the healing and delivering work of the Lord through faith in His Name.

God is able to heal any and all sickness and disease, and as a part of that, *God is able* to deliver from every bondage from which sickness and disease may arise. There is no disease, named or as yet un-named that He cannot heal. Regardless of where a disease falls in the alphabetical order of ailments, Jesus is Lord over it and has already made the provision for complete healing from it (Isaiah 53:4-5; Psalm 107:20; 1 Peter 2:24). Temporary or terminal, God is able to heal, and in fact, has already done the necessary work for it to be accomplished. Contagious or genetic, healing is not a problem for the Lord. Injury or natural onset, complete healing has already been purchased in full by the Lord. There is no method or means by which sickness might come over which Jesus cannot exercise power and bring complete healing. There is no place in which sickness can exist that the power of God cannot reach or is insufficient to bring complete healing. Let me state again and again until faith that cannot be stopped overcomes; *God is able to heal.* With all existing evidence, and with the knowledge that God cannot lie, be it known to all, *God is able to heal.* Let that be established in our hearts and minds as the first pillar in the foundational truth of our covenant of health.

...PILLAR NUMBER TWO...

Declaration of Will

As I stated earlier, I believe that every true Christian fully believes that God has the *ability* to heal, I must sadly state that *not* every true Christian believes it is God's *will* to heal. But let me leave no doubt here. It *is* God's will to heal. It always has been, is now, and as long as healing is needed, it always will be. Just as His ability is clearly seen throughout the Scriptures and throughout human history, so it is clearly seen throughout Scriptures and throughout human history that it is His will to heal. Again, let me state it clearly; *it is the will of God to heal.*

Just as both His Word and actions *demonstrate* His ability to heal, so both His Word and actions *declare* His *will* to *heal.* I draw your attention once again to all the recorded healings of Scripture, from the healing of an entire nation of Israel before their departure from Egypt, to the multiple references in the Gospels where we read that Jesus healed everyone present. Even to the prophetic times of the end where the trees on either side of the river of life each bore its fruit in its season, and the leaves were for the healing of the nations, we see His will declared. The Scriptures are clear; God has provided for His will in healing to be carried out in some way to every generation of mankind. He has *declared His will to heal.*

And lest there be a remaining question, I draw your attention (Matthew 8:3 & Mark 1:41) to the day Jesus had a leper come to Him, saying, that if Jesus wanted to do so, He could make him clean. Here we must remember the answer Jesus gave to him. Upon being approached by the leper and his question, Jesus responded definitively saying, "I will, be thou clean." And then having spoken, Jesus touched him and he was made clean from the leprosy. And to seal that statement into a Biblical and unchanging statement, add the words of Hebrews 13:8 where we read, "Jesus Christ the same yesterday, and today, and forever."

We read similar words about the Father in Malachi 3:6. There it states, "I am the Lord; I change not." With those two verses joined together, knowing that Father, Son, and Holy Ghost are One, and witnessing both the words and actions of Jesus to the leper, we can, in reality, draw only one reasonable conclusion. It is the *declared will of God to heal.* Jesus has declared it, and He and the Father are One in thought, action, will, purpose, and plan.

So, just as it should be established in the heart and mind of every believer that God has *demonstrated His ability to heal*, let it likewise be established in the heart and mind of every believer that God has, through the words of His Son, Jesus, *declared His will to heal.*

...PILLAR NUMBER THREE...

Determination of How

Now we come to the third pillar, and that is the *determination of how healing will come.* While we can be certain it will come from the Lord, the precise method by which it will come may not be known, and it is for that reason that we see some stumbling at this pillar. And the truth is, this really ought not be. That stumbling may arise from numerous elements.

We should in no way forget that one's faith can be a strong determinant of how the healing power of God may be manifest in one's life. The woman with the issue of blood said, "If I may but touch the hem of His garment." That became her point of contact, and that is always a key element in the work of healing. Jairus wanted Jesus to come to his house. The Roman Centurion desired only that Jesus speak the word. All these were points of contact, yet none of them attempted to force the Lord into a particular mode of action by which the healing they desired *must* come. It is to that point that I wish to speak.

I wonder how many people have thought or said, "Oh, if only Brother _________ can lay his hands on me; then I'll be healed." Or perhaps you've heard, "If I could just get a special word from Reverend __________, then I'll know what to do." Now don't misunderstand me. God can certainly use Brother _________ or Reverend __________ as agents to minister healing to someone. My question arises as to why anyone would limit the Lord in how He chooses to bring healing into one's life. I would never try to provoke anyone to pull back from using his faith in receiving the healing power of God. Use your faith. Use your knowledge of the Word of God. Honor Father in that, for without faith you cannot please Him. Allow your faith in Him to establish a point of contact, but open yourself, spirit, soul, and body, to allow Father to bring the healing you need into your life by any means He may choose. He certainly knows more about this than any of us.

Think on this. If I wanted to give you a million dollars, and you knew my ability to do so and my will to do so was absolutely true, how would you be willing to receive it? Would I have to give it to you in large bills, or small ones? Would I have to deposit it directly to your bank as a draft, or as a fund transfer? Would I have to give it to you directly, or would I have to use an intermediary? In truth, I don't think any of that would matter. All that would really matter is that I fulfilled my word to you and gave you the million dollars. You would be so glad to get it, that *how* it came would not make any difference, even if it came in coins. If it were a gift to me, all that would matter to me is that the one who promised it followed through on the promise.

Apply that same logic and thinking to healing. My friend, if I need healing in my body, I really don't care how it comes, as long as it comes. At the time of this writing, there are approximately 7.67 billion people on this planet. If we look at the details, I am convinced that Father has at least 7.67 billion ways to get healing to anyone believing Him for it. It could be . . .

- the fruit from a tree
- the leaves on the tree
- blood on a door post
- a roasted lamb
- looking on a brass serpent
- a tree branch dipped in water
- dipping in a muddy river
- turning to a wall and praying
- having someone spit in the eyes
- rubbing mud in the eyes
- spitting and touching a tongue

- sending the sick to a priest
- laying hands on the sick
- anointing the sick with oil
- the prayer of faith
- the prayer of agreement
- elders praying together
- and on and on goes the myriad of ways healing may come.

Once again, the main point here is that *how* one's healing comes should not be the primary concern of the person who needs healing. The main thing is that it comes, and the person who needs healing should not behave or think in a manner that limits God on how He heals, or puts Him into a box that reduces the choices Father has. My faith can, and in fact, often will, determine a specific point of contact by which healing will flow, and God honors such faith. Still, let us be mindful that the God Who made us knows more about how to bring healing into our lives than we will ever know. We must establish the four pillars of divine healing in our lives, believe them, and hold fast to them. But in doing that, we do not direct God in the *determination of how healing comes.* The child of God is owned by the great Creator God. Leave the wisdom of the *determination of how healing comes* to Him. Unlike our wildest and farthest-reaching imagination, He who can do far and abundantly above all we ask or think holds limitless potential in the *determination of how healing comes.*

...PILLAR NUMBER FOUR...

Destination of Manifestation

Coming to the fourth pillar, we enter into an arena related to healing that becomes deeply personal to each of us. Now we deal with the *destination of manifestation of healing.* In my heart, I am sure that having read this far, you certainly have strong faith in Father's *demonstration of ability to heal,* in His *declaration of will to heal,* and in His limitless *determination of how to heal.* All this is well and good, needful and appropriate.

Up to this point, we can speak of our faith in God in perhaps a broader sense that this should be a universal mindset as it regards our faith in God for healing. But now we step away from that somewhat universal mindset and address something that becomes very personal. Do *you* believe that the *destination of manifestation* is *you*? That, dear reader, is the key question as we come to the fourth pillar. Once again, *do you believe that the destination of manifestation is you?*

I cannot tell you how often I have encountered precious people whom Jesus loves, people for whom He suffered and died, people He has redeemed from the curse of the law, come to this point in the journey toward healing and health, only to pull back from the fullness of God's gift of healing. Too often they think that God will do it for others, but not for them. Perhaps they begin to think that they are unworthy. They remember something of their past, and have not fully committed their faith to 1 John 1:9. That precious verse of Scripture is so keenly important to the operation of our faith toward God and our ability to receive from Him.

My dear reader friend, if you are a child of God, and if you have sinned, you have an Advocate with Father, and His Name Jesus the Christ. And if you, as a child of God, have sinned, He is faithful and just to forgive your sin and cleanse you from all unrighteousness. That is so powerful in your life. Read it! Memorize it! Quote it to yourself often, especially if you sin! God *cannot lie*, and this verse is absolute truth. Here are some depths of this great truth that would serve any believer well to plant deeply within his/her spirit.

- When a Christian sins, he needs to confess the sin. Repentance may turn one from the sin, but it is the confession that removes the seed from his spirit.
- When the Christian confesses sin, Jesus if faithful (steadfast and never changing in His work or attitude) and just (fully authorized and operating according to absolutely legal position) to forgive (let it go and remember it no more) the sin, and cleanse (completely exonerate and wipe away) from all (every vestige of) that sin.
- When this happens, one is restored to full fellowship with Father as though sin never existed at all. That's called justification.

Therefore, my friend, you should fully understand, know, and embrace as your rightful position in Christ, that when you are cleansed by the blood of Jesus, you are no longer unworthy. Rather, you have been made completely worthy to receive every blessing of God. As a believer, you are the righteousness of God in Jesus Christ. Jesus has been made to be your wisdom, righteousness, sanctification, and redemption. It doesn't get any better than that.

That being true, there is nothing, no reason, no justification, that you should not be the sole *destination of manifestation of healing*. You, in Christ, are the place where healing comes to reside. Believe it, accept it, and walk in it to the glory of God.

Take a moment at this point to acknowledge the truth of God's Word over your life, especially as it relates to healing and health. Speak faith from your heart, and in so doing embrace these four pillars you have examined. Read the following words aloud, and allow faith to rise in your heart to a new level.

1. I know and am persuaded by the Word of God that my heavenly Father has made full and manifest *demonstration of His ability to heal.*
2. I know and am persuaded by the Word of God that my heavenly Father has made full and manifest *declaration of His will to heal.*
3. I yield my life to Him, being His child and His peculiar possession, and release my faith in Him, trusting Him fully for His chosen *determination of how healing will come.*
4. I know and am persuaded by the Word of God that because My Father has made me to be the righteousness of God in Christ, and has accepted me as His child, having grafted me into the Body of Christ, that I am the *destination of the manifestation of healing.*
5. *I am healed in Jesus's Name!*

CHAPTER FOURTEEN

If You Own It

The statement I am about to make is one that should be taken very seriously. If you own something, you are responsible for it. This is a universal principle, and is even upheld by the laws of most countries. For example, if I own property, I am responsible for its upkeep, appearance, and safety. If you are injured on my property, and my failure to maintain and secure the property can be shown as contributing to your injury, I can be held legally responsible. If I own an animal (horse, dog, cat, etc.), I am responsible for that animal's behavior. If my animal injures you, and that injury can be shown to be as a result of my failure to secure the animal, I can be held legally responsible.

If you own something, it is generally yours by purchase or gift, and regardless of the manner in which you received it, you are still responsible for it. If you buy a car and someone is injured while you are driving that car, you are responsible. If someone gives you a car, the same rules apply.

Now consider this question. What is it that has been gifted to you by covenant with Jehovah God? You belong to Him. But there are many things He has given you. Are you living responsibly?

Matthew 28:18-20

And Jesus came and spake unto them, saying, All power is given unto me in heaven and in earth. Go ye therefore, and teach all nations, baptizing them in the name of the Father, and of the Son, and of the Holy Ghost: Teaching them to observe all things whatsoever I have commanded you: and, lo, I am with you alway, even unto the end of the world. Amen.

Mark 16:15-18

And he said unto them, Go ye into all the world, and preach the gospel to every creature. He that believeth and is baptized shall be saved; but he that believeth not shall be damned. And these signs shall follow them that believe; In my name shall they cast out devils; they shall speak with new tongues; They shall take up serpents; and if they drink any deadly thing, it shall not hurt them; they shall lay hands on the sick, and they shall recover.

John 14:12-14

Verily, verily, I say unto you, He that believeth on me, the works that I do shall he do also; and greater works than these shall he do; because I go unto my Father. And whatsoever ye shall ask in my name, that will I do, that the Father may be glorified in the Son. If ye shall ask any thing in my name, I will do it.

2 Peter 1:2-4

Grace and peace be multiplied unto you through the knowledge of God, and of Jesus our Lord, According as his divine power hath given unto us all things that pertain unto life and godliness, through the knowledge of him that hath called us to glory and virtue: Whereby are given unto us exceeding great and precious promises: that by these ye might be partakers of the divine nature, having escaped the corruption that is in the world through lust.

If you own it, you are responsible for it. That statement will be the focus of this chapter. Read it again; if you own it, you are responsible for it. Let us consider one natural example – an automobile. You own it – you are responsible for it. Who . . .

- . . . legally determines who drives it? *You.*
- . . . is responsible for its maintenance? *You.*
- . . . is responsible (at least in the USA) to insure it? *You.*
- . . . determines the type of fuel used? *You.*
- . . . is responsible for its security? *You.*

I could continue on and on. The point is simple – if you own it, you are responsible for it.

Now let us consider that same scenario further. Could your car be stolen? Yes. If the thief crashes it, he may go to jail, but who is responsible for the repairs, or to finish paying for the car if it were not already completely paid-in-full? *You.* Could something happen to the car beyond your control, such as a fire, or a storm that destroys it? Yes. But if that happens, who is responsible for its repairs or for paying in full for the car? *You.* Once again, I say to you, if you own it, you are responsible for it.

One might say, "But I have insurance to take care of such possibilities." That is wonderful, but who is responsible for acquiring and paying for that insurance coverage? *You.* So, I'll say it again. If you own it, you are responsible for it. It's that simple. And it seems amazing to me that Christians all around the world understand this simple principle, but many of them don't seem to understand how it should be applied, even in their day-to-day walk as a Christian. In every believer's walk with the

Lord, he should fully realize that the truth of this statement *must* be applied in his life – *if you own it, you are responsible for it.*

Now let's carry our conversation to the next level. As a child of God, a Christian, a joint heir with Christ, and His ambassador, what do you own? My question does not relate to earthly possessions; houses, lands, vehicles, items purchased with money. My question is in relation to that which God has given specifically to you. Your answer would be in terms of talents, gifts, and anointings placed directly into your life by the hand of God (Father, Son, or and/or Holy Spirit). What elements of covenant has Father set forth into your life that He has declared belong to you?

In chapter one of Second Peter, verse 3, we read that Father has given you "all things that pertain to life and godliness." Note closely that He has "given" those things to you. If He gave them to you, they belong to you, not someone else. These are not elements that belong to Him that He is allowing you to use. These are "things" that He has "given" to you. They belong to you. You own them. Remember, now, *if you own it, you are responsible for it.*

Now let's draw our focus, not away from the principle of which I write, but more so on healing and health. What has Father, Son, and Holy Spirit given to each believer as it relates to healing and health? Let's look as closely at that as our space will permit in this writing. And let us take that look through the lens of the Word of God, for God and His Word are One, Jesus is the Word made flesh, and Holy Spirit is the giver of the Word to mankind. What does the Word of God say?

While we in no way have space to give an exhaustive reference of all healing Scriptures, there are some that are key to our needed understanding of ownership as it relates to healing and health. Let us take a deeper and more intentional look at some of these powerful passages.

Exodus 23:25

And ye shall serve the LORD your God, and he shall bless thy bread, and thy water; and I will take sickness away from the midst of thee.

Note the words, "I will take sickness away from the midst of thee." In the English language, there is no stronger word of affirmation of intent than *will* or *shall*. When one says, "I will," that should settle all discussion. If one says, "I will," and does not, one is a liar, and we know that God cannot lie (Hebrews 6:18). For the child of God, that should make this passage easy to accept, for it was God Who was speaking.

Note, too, the tense of what was said. "I will" signifies an element of the future. Keep in mind that this was spoken in the Old Covenant, the New Covenant had not yet been set in place, and Father was, therefore, making a promise of intended purpose. A promise is a statement of intended purpose in the future, to either do, or to not do a certain thing. Here, Father said "I will take sickness away from the midst of thee." Therefore, His statement here was a promise of something He would fully establish at some point in the future. The question then is, has that promise been fulfilled, and if so, when? Keep in mind here that until Jesus conquered sin, death, hell, and Satan, and established the New Covenant, Satan was the owner/operator of the world, because Adam, upon his transgression in the garden of Eden, gave it all to Satan.

Psalm 103:1-4

Bless the LORD, O my soul: and all that is within me, *bless* his holy name.

Bless the LORD, O my soul, and forget not all his benefits:

Who forgiveth all thine iniquities; who healeth all thy diseases;

Who redeemeth thy life from destruction; who crowneth thee with lovingkindness and tender mercies;

Here we are still examining the Word of the Lord set forth in the Old Covenant (Old Testament). For that reason, I ask you to focus for a moment on possession. It may seem a minor point, but it truly is not. In this text, we are told to "forget not all his benefits." So, at the time of this writing, whose benefits are the forgiveness of all iniquities, the healing of all diseases, the redeeming of life from destruction, and crowning with lovingkindness and tender mercies? In this passage it is clearly stated that these benefits belong to the Lord. He bestowed them upon His people in the Old Covenant, but they still belonged to Him.

Still, this should cause great joy in the heart of a New Testament believer. If Father was willing to bestow His possessions upon people who were *not* born again, and even in some cases upon people who did not even have covenant with Him, how blessed should we of the New Covenant consider ourselves that we have stepped into an arena of forgiveness, healing, redemption, and blessing that was as yet *unknown* in the Old Covenant?

Also, we need to once again look at the tense of the language that was used. The tense used here is present tense for those to whom it was given at that time, but we should not forget the possession factor. All these benefits still were the possession of Father God, and as yet had not been released to the possession of someone else. In fact, because men of the Old Covenant were children of the devil and *not* sons of God, Father could not release His benefits into the possession of someone who belonged to Satan. Yet, while still His benefits, He loved so much that He made these blessings available to people who, at that time, were as yet not His children. What a great love!

Psalm 107:20

He sent his word, and healed them, and delivered *them* from their destructions.

Now make no mistake about it. We can find places throughout the Old Testament where Father healed people, even entire nations of people. And this passage we now examine has been shown to be truth again and again throughout the history of God's people, whether it be Israel or the Church. Let it be forever known that God sent His Word and healed and delivered.

But with this verse, I want to draw your attention, not for distraction, but for a sharp focus, to the first chapter of John. There we read that the Word became flesh and dwelled among us. That Word was Jesus in the flesh. Now consider this. From the day of Adam's fall in the garden, Father started the work of sending His Word into the earth. In the Garden He said that the "seed of the woman" (that would be Jesus) would bruise the head of the serpent (that would be Satan), and that Satan would bruise the heel of the woman's seed (Genesis 3:15). From that moment in the garden of Eden, the seed was being planted that would culminate in the birth of Jesus to the virgin Mary. And in order for that birth to occur, Mary came into agreement with what the angel of the Lord told her, and she said, "be it unto me according to your word" (Luke 1:38). It was that moment in which the "fulness of time" (Galatians 4:4) took place, and the Word of God (Jesus in the flesh) was conceived in Mary's womb. From that point until His resurrection from the dead, Jesus was working to fulfill the text we examine here, Psalm 107:20. Jesus, the fulness of the Word, had come and redeemed us from the curse of the law. The Word (Jesus in the flesh) had been sent, and He had done the full work of redemption, including all that was necessary for the new birth, healing, deliverance, and provision (Galatians 3:13-29). And when that work was accomplished, healing (and the fullness of redemption) was no longer a possession of the Lord that He made manifest in us. Rather it became our possession, and becoming our possession, we have now come into a place of responsibility for that possession.

Proverbs 4:20-22

My son, attend to my words; incline thine ear unto my sayings.

Let them not depart from thine eyes; keep them in the midst of thine heart.

For they *are* life unto those that find them, and health to all their flesh.

Once again, I ask you to look at this passage with a focus on the tense of the statements made. Everything in this passage is present tense. It speaks to action, *now*; maintenance of function, *now*; and results, *now*. And because it is all about now, it must therefore be ongoing. It is not about giving attention to the Word *once*, for when that moment is past, it is no longer *now*.

The full implication of this passage should be clear. If we are to enjoy the benefits of *life* to our whole being and *health* to our entire body, we must diligently take up the work of giving our attention to the Word of God consistently, daily, throughout our life. That would give us easy reference to Joshua 1:8. Read it here – "This book of the law shall not depart out of thy mouth; but thou shalt meditate therein day and night, that thou mayest observe to do according to all that is written therein: for then thou shalt make thy way prosperous, and then thou shalt have good success." If one is to enjoy the blessing of covenant with Jehovah God, one must accept certain responsibilities that cannot be cast off, avoided, or passed on to another.

Isaiah 53:4-5

Surely he hath borne our griefs, and carried our sorrows: yet we did esteem him stricken, smitten of God, and afflicted.

But he *was* wounded for our transgressions, *he was* bruised for our iniquities: the chastisement of our peace *was* upon him; and with his stripes we are healed.

While our primary focus in this discussion is ownership, here we still consider the tense of the verbiage used. This passage is particularly poignant regarding that issue. Note that Jesus "hath borne our griefs …. carried our sorrows …. was wounded for our transgressions …. was bruised for our iniquities …. chastisement of our peace was upon him" …. all that is past tense. Now look at the final statement in this text; "with his stripes we are healed" (present tense). This is a particularly poignant revelation. The elements to which the past tense is applied are all elements of our personal relationship with Father having to do with cleansing from transgression and iniquity, and peace through reconciliation. All those are past tense, and need to be in place before we can receive as our personal possession the healing in the Covenant.

This is not to say that even unbelievers cannot be healed by the power of God. However, we need to realize that when healing takes place *outside* covenant, it is God *doing* something *for* someone. But when healing takes place *inside* covenant, it is a result of something Father has *already given* us; something that is already our possession.

Matthew 8:16-17

When the even was come, they brought unto him many that were possessed with devils: and he cast out the spirits with *his* word, and healed all that were sick:

That it might be fulfilled which was spoken by Esaias the prophet, saying, Himself took our infirmities, and bare *our* sicknesses.

When Jesus healed Peter's mother-in-law, and did all the healing that followed that same day, He was still operating as a prophet under the Old Covenant. He was giving those present a foretaste of that which was to come in the New Covenant. At that moment in time, the New Covenant was not yet in place, and would not be until He was raised from the dead, seated on the right hand of His Father, and had sent Holy Spirit on the day of Pentecost. He wanted those about Him to have a glimpse of what Isaiah had prophesied.

Now look at verse 17 of the passage in question. The words written here are powerfully forceful words. We read the statement, "Himself took our infirmities, and bare *our* sicknesses." Two words stand out in their forcefulness; took and bare. Jesus did not *ask* for our infirmities, nor did He *merely aid* in carrying them. He *took* our infirmities, and *bare* our sicknesses.

The word *took* implies that this was a forceful wrenching of *our* infirmities from us, and that He *bare* our sicknesses speaks to a full and complete carrying away of sickness from us. That being true, that *our* infirmities and *our* sicknesses have been forcefully removed and carried away from us, then what shall we call the infirmities and sicknesses that we encounter now under the New Covenant? Do you see it? Jesus *took our* infirmities and *bare our* sicknesses. Therefore, that which we encounter *now* are no longer ours, but are lies of the enemy brought to us in an attempt to entangle us in a yoke of bondage from which we have already been redeemed.

In my writing, I am in no way denying the existence of sickness, disease, or infirmity. What I *am* stating is that what the believer encounters does not belong to him, but is nothing less than an attack of the enemy.

Acts 10:38

How God anointed Jesus of Nazareth with the Holy Ghost and with power: who went about doing good, and healing all that were oppressed of the devil; for God was with him.

Before moving into direct commentary on this passage, I encourage you to take a moment to read the opening words of Jesus found in Luke 4:18. Pay close attention to what Jesus said, the verbiage, and the tenses of the verbs used. Jesus said, "The Spirit of the Lord is upon Me because He hath anointed Me…."

Once again, I urge you to closely consider what the Lord said in this passage. Jesus said, "The Spirit of the Lord" (that is Holy Ghost) "IS" (present tense of a passive verb indicating current state of condition) "upon Me because" (the word "because" indicates that there is a specific reason for Holy Spirit's being upon Him) "He hath" (this is past tense; clear indication here that Holy Spirit's presence of power [dunamis] was preceded by something else) "anointed Me." (there is truly no way around this conclusion – anointing precedes power [dunamis]).

Using the same words, and without any attempt to change meaning, read this passage in this way; "Because He hath anointed Me, the Spirit of the Lord is upon Me." (my rendering) It should be so very clear to us. What God anoints, God empowers when that anointing is yielded to Him. If you want the power of God in your life, yield to Him that which He has anointed in your life. Don't expect God's power to be manifest in your life in an arena in which you are *not* anointed.

1 Peter 2:24

Who his own self bare our sins in his own body on the tree, that we, being dead to sins, should live unto righteousness: by whose stripes ye were healed.

What a joy it is to read this passage of Scripture! This revelation in God's Word takes Isaiah 53:5 to an entirely new level. It moves the prophetic of Isaiah to a present state of being that belongs to the child of God. This passage begins in speaking to the issue of spiritual life and relationship with the Lord. Because Jesus "bare our sins in His Own body," we no longer have to carry them. The manner in which it is stated should make that clear. Man carries about in himself the sin nature as a child of Satan until he is born again. At the moment of the new birth, "old things pass away and all things become new" (2 Corinthians 5:17-21). This doesn't have to happen over and over; just once. And that happens when we confess with our mouth that Jesus Christ is Lord and believe in our heart that God has raised Him from the dead (Romans 10:9-10).

But this time, when we come to the issue of healing for the body, unlike Isaiah 53:5, the tense of the statement has changed. In Isaiah we read, "with His stripes we are healed," but here in 1 Peter 2:24, we read, "by Whose stripes ye were healed." Now, having come fully into the New Covenant, we have moved from a present tense state of being that was by the power of God to a past tense action resulting in a current state of being. And once again I reiterate, just as with the element of reconciliation with God and spiritual new birth, this state of healing is not one that has to be wrought over and over again. Rather, it is a state of being healed that was not only wrought for us by the Lord Jesus, but which has been conferred upon us by Him as a part of our heritage as children of God.

Once again, I draw your attention to the fact that in the Old Covenant, God demonstrated His ability to heal, declared His will to heal through His actions, unfolded His love for mankind by His multitudinous determinations of how healing could come, and made it clear that His destination for healing was mankind. But in all He did in the Old Covenant, His healing was a demonstration of His ability, love, and character. It all belonged to Him.

But in the New Covenant, things have changed. When Jesus was raised from the dead and declared to be Lord by our heavenly Father, healing became a settled issue belonging to the believer; no longer a promise. I know, so many people think of healing as a promise. But remember, a promise is a statement concerning some future action. But now, in the church age, in the New Covenant, it's no longer a promise, but a settled fact. It belongs to the believer. We now own it. And *if you own it, you are responsible for it.*

CHAPTER FIFTEEN

Responsibility Expressed

As previously stated, when you own something, you are responsible for it. God owns His children, and He accepts full responsibility for them to provide all they need in life. He has declared that we are to "seek first the kingdom of God, and all these things shall be added unto you" (Matthew 6:33). Those "things" to which He refers are food, clothes, and shelter, the basic necessities of life. And He furthermore said that this would be the case for those of "little faith" (Matthew 6:30). All this is laid out in Matthew 6. Because He owns us, He is responsible for us.

But when we speak of healing, we speak of a gift, a possession given to us by our Lord through His work of redemption. Eternal life belongs to you. You are responsible to live it and demonstrate it. Peace of mind belongs to you. You are responsible to live it and demonstrate it. Healing and health belong to you. You are responsible to live it and demonstrate it.

Sadly, many believers don't know this. It's time the church realized what belongs to it, and how it is to live in and demonstrate that ownership. Accept your responsibility.

Joshua 1:8

This book of the law shall not depart out of thy mouth;
but thou shalt meditate therein day and night,
that thou mayest observe to do according to all that is written
therein: for then thou shalt make thy way prosperous,
and then thou shalt have good success.

Proverbs 4:20-23

My son, attend to my words; incline thine ear unto my sayings. Let them not depart from thine eyes; keep them in the midst of thine heart. For they are life unto those that find them, and health to all their flesh. Keep thy heart with all diligence; for out of it are the issues of life.

Matthew 7:24-27

Therefore whosoever heareth these sayings of mine, and doeth them, I will liken him unto a wise man, which built his house upon a rock: And the rain descended, and the floods came, and the winds blew, and beat upon that house; and it fell not: for it was founded upon a rock.

And every one that heareth these sayings of mine, and doeth them not, shall be likened unto a foolish man, which built his house upon the sand: And the rain descended, and the floods came, and the winds blew, and beat upon that house; and it fell: and great was the fall of it.

John 14:15-17

If ye love me, keep my commandments. And I will pray the Father, and he shall give you another Comforter, that he may abide with you for ever; Even the Spirit of truth; whom the world cannot receive, because it seeth him not, neither knoweth him: but ye know him; for he dwelleth with you, and shall be in you.

Healing belongs to the believer. That's the simple truth of the matter. The real work for the believer is not in procuring that healing, for that work has already been done in the redemptive work of Jesus. The real work of the believer as it relates to healing and health is the work of exercising responsibility for that healing and health.

God is a Triune Being; God the Father, God the Son, and God the Holy Ghost. He made man in His image, and one of the elements of the image is that man, too, is a triune being; spirit, soul, and body. The spirit is the real person; that part of man that can have direct communion with the Godhead; Father, Son, and Holy Ghost. The soul is that element of man in which he reasons, thinks, and accesses human emotions by which "feelings" can be expressed. The body is the earth suit in which all that is contained. It is made of the flesh and its five sensory elements; sight, hearing, taste, smell, and touch.

Again, in this chapter, I do not intend my writing to be considered exhaustive, but to set forth some practical guidelines that, if followed, can serve to put one on a forward and upward moving track by which one can receive healing manifest in their body and move steadily toward the realization of full ownership of the healing and health that belongs to every believer. Let's look at these guidelines in the three arenas of human life where they should be applied.

Spirit

The spirit man is the real you. You *are* a spirit, you *have* a soul, and you *live* in a body. Here we focus on the spirit man. Feed yourself daily, diligently, and deliberately on the Word of God. It requires faith to please God, and it requires faith to move God (Hebrews 11:6). Faith comes by hearing, and hearing by the Word of God (Romans 10:17). The Word of God feeds your spirit, feeds you faith, and is itself the seed of God by which the entire kingdom of God operates (Mark 4).

Read the Word, listen to the Word, study the Word, meditate upon the Word, memorize the Word, speak the Word at all times in all situations, hide the Word in your heart, and allow the Word to be life to you and health to all your flesh. Put the Word first place in your life, and give it final authority over all you say and do. The Word will light your path and be a lamp to your feet. The Word is settled forever in heaven, the Word is the power of God unto salvation, and it is the Word by which Father is upholding all things. Use the Word as your clothing, for every article of the armor of God is fully Word-based. The Word is the Water of life, the Bread of life, and in fact, IS your life. Hold fast to the Word, allow *nothing* to take it from you, and keep your spirit-man filled with the Word.

There is an undisputable, unalterable, unchanging, and unbreakable connection to the Word of God in your spirit, and healing and health in your body. Acknowledge that bond, hold fast to it, for as we have read previously, the Word of God is "life to those who find it and health to all their flesh" (Proverbs 4:22). Hold fast to the Word, for it is the washing of the water by the Word that serves to help keep you clean before the Lord, and therefore in a position to receive the manifestation of healing and health in your life. Healing and health are elements of the kingdom of God that belong to you, and the entire kingdom of God operates on the seed principle of the Word of God.

Soul

The soul is comprised of the mind, will, intellect, and emotions. They all have distinct functions, yet they all function together as a unit. It is the Word of God that, when applied to this complex realm of operations, can bring about the kind of orderly function that is truly creative, constructive, and congruent with life that needs to be lived and exhibited. Think of the soulish realm in the following manner.

The mind is the operation's center. It needs a properly balanced power supply and atmospheric controls that enable the systems to function at their maximum output. The Word of God is that power supply and creates the proper atmospheric conditions for optimum performance. The will is the decision-making center. It needs properly selected and accurate data to supply the decision-making elements with all necessary resources to receive, filter, and utilize input for optimum outcome. The Word of God is that light of selection and the filter that ensures clean and accurate decisions. The intellect is the storage center where data, knowledge, and information are gathered and stored, and become available for future decisions and operations. The Word of God is the filtering, arranging, and storage control resource that ensures clean storage, proper arrangement for optimal access, and by the washing of the water of the Word, keeps the storage clean and undefiled by external pollution and contaminants. And finally, the emotions are human emissions. In the industry of the soul, as in the industry of the world, it is necessary that the fuels and energy supply that is used be as clean as possible, producing emissions that are not harmful to the surrounding atmosphere. The Word of God is that fuel for the soul, feeding it, filtering input, producing creative output, and controlling the emissions to give needed and pleasing relief to the soul of a man while guarding against pollution.

The Word of God makes up the "whole armor of God" as described in Ephesians 6:11. And among those elements of clothing is the "helmet of salvation" (Ephesians 6:17). That is protection for the head, often thought of as the seat of the soul. There is the "breastplate of righteousness" (Ephesians 6:14), being "girt about the loins with truth" (Ephesians 6:14). That is protection for the heart (or spirit) of man. Having one's feet "shod with the preparation of the Gospel of peace" (Ephesians 6:15) sets forth an image of having one's day-to-day walk in life protected. And let us not forget the "shield of faith" (Ephesians 6:16), the filter system, the protection against the fiery darts of Satan that are used against the whole man; spirit, soul, and body. And of course, there is the "sword of the Spirit" (Ephesians 6:17), which is the Word of God, that proceeds forth in the words we speak.

And it is in the words that come from our mouths that our mental processes are brought to light. It is from those words that our will becomes known, and that our intellect is, in large part, revealed. And by those words, the emissions of our life flow into the world about us. Oh, the power of those words. And with something so powerful flowing from us, it is only right and proper that we apply to our soulish life a power, a life, a revelation, an insight, an enlightenment, and a fuel source that produces that which is good from our life. And that element of which I write is the Word of God.

But where our soul (mind, will, intellect, and emotions) is concerned, there are other things we must consider. Don't remain ignorant. Learn all you can learn. Feed you intellect with truly useful knowledge. A quality education can be a marvelous tool for life. Learn about relationships with people, human interactions, and how we can interact with others to the greatest advantage of everyone about us.

Perhaps the key reason for delving into learning about the business of relationships is that no one knows everything. A few people know a great deal about a few things. Don't concern yourself with being well-rounded in life. You don't have time for that. Seek rather to be well-surrounded by good people who know what you do not know. Finding such people and establishing relationships with them is one of your paramount safety nets in life. The Word of God will be your greatest resource for learning how to create, establish, and nurture those valuable relationships. So, again I say to you, go to the Word to build and establish a sound soulish life.

Body

Now we speak of the body; our earth suit. The body is our badge of authority to live and move about in this life as we choose. Just as one needs a space suit to survive in space, so one needs an earth suit to carry out life as we know it. That is perhaps the greatest reason Satan has for desiring to possess the human being. The human body gives him abilities he does not otherwise have. Jesus has stripped him of his power and authority, and the only way he can exercise real power and authority in the earth is if a human being, someone in an earth suit, yields their rightful place, power, and authority to him. This is also the reason the Scriptures teach us that to be absent from the body is to be present with the Lord. God will not allow a disembodied spirit to run free in the earth. The chaos that could cause is beyond discovery.

The body is the temple of Holy Ghost. Holy Ghost is the third Person of the Trinity. He is God, and as such, should merit a place of honor in which to dwell. It should be the goal of every believer to provide Holy Ghost with a temple of honor, sanctified and meet for the Master's use. That temple should be one that is strong, well, and able to be used at the highest level. I believe God wants the temple of Holy Ghost to be well, whole, healed, healthy. So, where the physical body is concerned, the believer should be aware of the condition of his body, and should seek to maintain that body as it lies within his ability, to honor the Lord in properly tending to the body.

One should guard the body against unnecessary damages by avoiding foolish endeavors and refraining from engaging in activities that are unwise. One should seek to maintain a high level of fitness for the body so it can serve the Lord and the person who lives in it well. That means that one should engage in some productive type of regular physical exercise. That could be walking or jogging, and many other forms of fitness training, not the least of which are sports activities of many kinds.

If something is wrong in your body, and you know it, but you don't know what it is, have a good medical doctor examine you. True faith does not work like a shot in the dark, hoping you somehow hit something accurately. When the problem has been accurately identified, it can be more accurately dealt with by faith. It should be understood that the mountain of which Jesus spoke in Mark 11 was not some non-descript issue, but a specific one that had been properly identified. Don't fear doctors or the medical community. God can use them. But at all times, against all odds, and facing every situation, use your faith, for faith brings God on the scene.

Watch your diet. Overeating, non-nutritional eating, over-indulgence in what some would call *junk food*, and eating knowingly undercooked or improperly cooked foods should be avoided. While you cannot always determine what will be set before you, you should use good judgment concerning foods that you can control. I travel internationally doing leadership training, and often find myself in a place where I am a bit uncertain about what I am eating. In those times and places, my faith in God becomes my sustaining life force. But for me to be in a place where I have control, and to deliberately eat a quart of ice cream, or eat gluttonously of any meal, and especially to eat heavily just before bedtime would be utterly foolish on my part, deliberately injurious to my health, and a poor witness of someone who should be doing all things in moderation.

There are many other areas I could address in this chapter, but I will leave that to your good sense and basic understanding. I will refer to an earlier statement. While you do indeed belong to God, your body is your responsibility to maintain. Your soul falls to your responsibility to train, teach, and use properly. The real you, the spirit man, is your responsibility to guard, feed, and make the necessary choices for life. And, my friend, *if you own it, you are responsible for it.*

CHAPTER SIXTEEN

In Remembrance . . .

In this second edition of Covenant of Health – Beyond a Promise, I have not only made some editing changes, but have added three new chapters. Chapter Five, "Whose House Is It?," Chapter Eleven, "Only Candidates Get Elected," and this concluding chapter, "In Remembrance . . ." I believe they will add so much to this second edition.

This final chapter focuses on Communion. This writing took place after a period of almost five months of personally taking Communion in my private worship. So much has been revealed to me in this time, that at this writing I fully intend to continue this practice throughout the remainder of this year. These personal times with the Lord have been enriching beyond my ability to communicate it. Still, there is much I want to share with you to make Covenant of Health – Beyond a Promise become even more powerful and alive in your life. Be blessed, and may you hear the voice of the Lord singing over you with joy.

Matthew 26:26-28

And as they were eating, Jesus took bread, and blessed it,
and brake it, and gave it to the disciples, and said,
Take, eat; this is my body.
And he took the cup, and gave thanks, and gave it to them,
saying, Drink ye all of it;
For this is my blood of the new testament,
which is shed for many for the remission of sins.

1 Corinthians 11:23-30

For I have received of the Lord that which also I delivered unto you, That the Lord Jesus the same night in which he was betrayed took bread:And when he had given thanks, he brake it, and said, Take, eat: this is my body, which is broken for you: this do ***in remembrance*** *of me.*

After the same manner also he took the cup, when he had supped, saying, This cup is the new testament in my blood: this do ye, as oft as ye drink it, ***in remembrance*** *of me.*

For as often as ye eat this bread, and drink this cup, ye do shew the Lord's death till he come. Wherefore whosoever shall eat this bread, and drink this cup of the Lord, unworthily, shall be guilty of the body and blood of the Lord.

But let a man examine himself, and so let him eat of that bread, and drink of that cup. For he that eateth and drinketh unworthily, eateth and drinketh damnation to himself, not discerning the Lord's body. For this cause many are weak and sickly among you, and many sleep.

As the close of 2020 neared, having experienced what I believe to be one of the most critical years the body of Christ had ever experienced, at least in my lifetime, and I believe in the history of our nation, I determined to pursue the Lord to greater depths than I had ever known. And that determination was the strongest I have ever known in my life as a believer. There were things I yet needed to know, to understand, and to have revealed to me by Holy Spirit. The search was on.

What was called the Corona virus, or COVID-19 appeared to become a very costly pandemic, not only economically, but in human lives and suffering, too. Political, racial, international, economic, and social upheaval rocked billions of human lives. My purpose here is not to recite the history of that year, but to point to the fact that something in the Church was evidently wrong. I will not single our any denomination, or any single church. But I will say, and that unapologetically, something was gravely wrong in the Church.

The Church is the body of Christ, and Jesus is the head of His Church. He is Lord over His Church. He is Savior, Healer, Deliverer, Provider, and Lord Advocate General of His Church. Yet it seemed in so many ways that much of our Lord's Church was powerless against the myriad of fiery darts that were fired at the Church during 2020.

My heart was crying out for answers. I knew those answers were to be found in the Word of God, and would be discovered in study, meditation, and obedience to the Word, and prayer and communion with Father, our Lord, and Holy Spirit. As I searched my own heart, and tried to view all that was happening through the eyes of the Lord, one thing kept coming into my heart. Communion!

When I studied, I thought of Communion. When I prayed, I thought of Communion. When I fellowshipped with dear fellow saints, I thought of Communion.

Especially during the month of November, 2020, Communion was constantly on my mind. For the first ten days of that month, I partook of Communion in my personal time with the Lord. On November 11, my bride and I both tested positive for COVID. But that is where our story differs from so many. She had a minor ache or two, and coughed a bit for a day or so. All that happened to me was loss of taste for about four days. That was it. You see, I had put into practice the preceding chapters of this book. I had studied the Word and learned to live it and walk it out daily.

I knew that COVID was real. I knew it was in our community. I knew the enemy would use it to come after me. He always lives up to his John 10:10 identity. But I also knew how to handle a thief.

If I am in my own home, and a thief breaks in to steal from me, harm me, and destroy what he cannot steal, he is in for a rude awakening. I will not sit idly by and allow that to happen. I will meet him at the door with far superior force, resist him with all my might, skill, and weaponry, and leave his bloody carcass outside my home. I will do the same thing for my bride of 50 years.

I hold that same attitude towards any thief, including those who operate in the realm of the spirit. Once again, I knew the enemy would bring COVID against me as a weapon. But the weapons of my warfare are not carnal. They are powerful, sharp, and ready for use. And further, without intending to boast, I have learned to use them, I can say with King David that my God has taught my hands to war, and has made me skillful in the use of the weapons of my warfare. So, when the enemy came to my door, I did not hide and wish he would go away. I met him with the full force and violence of the weapons of God. Yes, there was a fight. Yes, there was (spiritual) bloodletting and violence. And yes, I won, for I am more than a conqueror; I am an overcomer by faith in Christ. No doctors, no special medication, no hospital, no bedtime, no breakdown. Jesus is my Lord, and to Him and Him alone will I bow my knee. Sometimes you have to fight to keep what belongs to you. There you have my testimony over Satan and COVID. That, too, became a part of my thinking as I moved toward 2021.

So, I asked the Lord what I personally needed to do. He directed me to Communion. It was then, in December, 2020, I made my commitment to the Lord to take Communion each day of 2021 as a part of my daily time with Him. I have taken time for that every day, beginning January 1, 2021, and on some days have been directed to come to the Lord's table a second time. I have added Communion to almost every encounter with fellow believers in my office. These times proved to be enriching beyond description, revelatory beyond all I could have imagined, and inspiringly deepening in my personal relationship with the Lord and understanding of His Word.

As I prayed and meditated over the Word and daily practice of Communion, I asked the Lord to unfold for me all the significance of Communion I could handle. I'm sure there is more than I can write here, and I am still seeking after it. But here, I am sharing what I received to this point.

- The Bread -

One of the first things I saw, something I had never deeply considered, was the words of Paul in which Jesus said, ". . . this do *in remembrance* of me . . ." Two of those words jumped out at me in a way I had never seen them. ". . . *in remembrance* . . ." Partaking of Communion was not something about the future. It was all about remembering what Jesus has already done. With that in mind, let us engage in some Biblical remembering.

When Paul wrote First Corinthians, he said that Jesus told us that receiving Communion should be done "*in remembrance*" of Him. The earthly work of Jesus was finished when He hung on the cross on Golgotha. There Jesus said it Himself, "It is finished." His full work was not finished, for He ever lives to make intercession according to the will of Father. His earthly work, however, was done. When Jesus gathered His disciples around Him at the table of the last supper, He took one of the loaves of bread used in the Passover Feast, He broke that bread, and He said to His disciples, "Take, eat: this is my body, which is broken for you: this do *in remembrance* of me." Note closely what took place at that moment.

- Jesus gave a command to do something. He told them to "take" and "eat" the bread He gave them.
- Jesus identified what the bread represented. It was His body broken for them.
- Jesus told them why they were doing this. It was to be done *in remembrance* of Him; Who He was, what He did, and what He provided.

We see that phrase again – *in remembrance* of Him. To remember is to think upon something that has already taken place; a past event. In this case, what had taken place was the willing sacrifice Jesus made of Himself through His broken body for the healing of all who would make Him Lord. Note that I said "all who would make Him Lord." As we read in Romans 10:9-10, if you will confess that Jesus is Lord, and believe in your heart that God raised Him from the dead, you shall be saved. This is not stated as a maybe, or a possibility, or something for only a select number. This is a whosoever statement we see in Romans 10:13. There it plainly states that "whosoever shall call upon the Name of the Lord shall be saved." And my friend, if you're a whosoever, that includes you.

When we read the word "saved," we are talking about a Greek word "sozo." That is an all-encompassing term that covers much more than the new birth. It references not only the new birth, but the renewing of the mind, the healing of the body, deliverance from all evil, and abundant provision of every need. But what is amazing, it seems that most people who believe in the all-encompassing work still hold back from accepting all it provides.

When you are born again, what are the primary adjectives that describes the life you receive at that point? Two words come to mind; everlasting or eternal. They both mean the same thing. The life that you receive when you are born again is "everlasting life." That is the life that is given to anyone who believes on Jesus. That is clearly set forth in one of the most familiar passages of Scripture in the Bible; John 3:16.

Now consider this. If the life you receive at the new birth is "everlasting" life, or "eternal" life, why would anything else that comes with the new birth be in any way temporary? When I was born again, I received eternal, or everlasting life. I also received the capacity to renew my mind in the manifest form of the mind of Christ. Was that a temporary gift, or is that my eternal gift, too? It, too, is eternal, or everlasting.

Let's look further. Is the deliverance I receive at the new birth temporary, or is it, too, eternal, or everlasting. Once again, it is eternal. And what of abundance of provision? My friend, it, too, is eternal, or everlasting.

That being the case, we come to the matter of healing. Healing is a definite part of salvation. When I received salvation, I also received the capacity for a renewed mind into which I can constantly tap, deliverance from all evil, and the abundant provision of every need. And when I received salvation, I also received my healing. And having received my healing, I was thereafter healed. Ah, but as Shakespeare would say, "there's the rub." That is where we have such difficulty. But why? I believe it falls into two categories.

First, it is difficult for us to grasp because we simply haven't been taught the Word of God as it pertains to our health. Secondly, because it focuses so much on the physical body, our physical senses become tools with which Satan can play havoc when we base our belief on our feelings and not on the Word of God.

(Think of this. How long did Father intend Adam [male and female] to live in the garden? Forever. But when sin entered, so did death, and along with it, soulish torment, sickness, bondage,

and lack (poverty). But how long did Adam live after he committed high treason and was put out of the garden. He lived for 930 years [Genesis 5]. How is it that a mortal man could live to be 930 years of age? I believe it was because he did not know how to die. I am convinced that it took him 930 years to learn that. And for a number of generations, man lived to be extremely old. I find it very interesting that until the last century, the age of men seemed to grow shorter and shorter until they began to learn how to live again. While many people attribute such to science, once again, I believe the primary reason was the outpouring of Holy Ghost after the turn of the 20th century as the Lord began to prepare His church for the coming of the Lord.)

My friend, just as the life one receives when salvation comes is eternal, so are all the remaining elements of that salvation, and that includes healing. Please allow your mind to simply think through the process. Sadly, we have been trained to believe that while we receive eternal life, that our healing is, at best, temporary. We have come to believe that the power of Satan, sickness, and disease is so great that it can take from us the divine health that Jesus gave us, and that we must therefore go back to Father again and again to get more healing. Dear one, nothing is further from the truth.

Since you have been born again, have there ever been times when Satan has sorely tempted you to believe that you really never received salvation? Certainly, and probably often. But if you have filled your heart and mind with the Word of God, and hold fast to it, you know that such temptation is a lie, and you refuse to accept it and allow it to drag you down.

Why then do so many Christians allow Satan to use symptoms as a temptation to believe their health has been taken away from them, and sickness and disease has replaced it? Why do so many Christians believe they have to go back to Father again and again to be healed? You don't have to return to Father to be saved over and over. Why can't we believe and hold fast to the truth that healing became ours at the new birth? Yes, symptoms and feelings come, and they come powerfully. But instead of believing we have lost our health, why can we not choose rather to fight to keep our health, knowing that Father gave it to us to be as eternal as the life He gave us?

Allow me to continue. When I was born again, I received eternal life, and I have to fight the good fight of faith to live it and model it daily. By the same token, when I received eternal life, I also received eternal health. If, the moment before I was born again, I was spiritually dead, and the moment of the new birth gave me eternal life, then the moment after I was born again, I was a possessor of eternal life. The same must hold true for healing and health. If the moment before I was born again, sickness could rule my flesh for Satan who was my lord, then the moment I was born again, I received healing from any sickness and disease, and the moment after I was born again, having received healing, I was healed, and that eternally.

Now, after I have been born again, just as Father intended that I should enjoy eternal life, He likewise intended that I enjoy the mind of Christ eternally, deliverance for eternity, and abundant provision for eternity. So, too, He intended for me to enjoy eternal health. It is simply part of the New Covenant and the life provided through it. And in every arena of my salvation provision, having received all that Father provided, I must learn to recognize what Father has given, how to enjoy what Father has given, and how to fight for and keep what Father has given. Just as Naboth refused to sell his inherited possession to King Ahab (1 Kings 21), so I refuse to allow Satan to take my inherited possession from me by any means. I will fight with all that is in me to keep it. That is a major element of the good fight of faith; fighting to keep what God has given you. And you can win!

On June 17, 1959, at about 8:30 PM, in a small church in Pinnacle, North Carolina, I received Jesus as my Lord and Savior. A moment before, I was a child of Satan. I belonged to him and without knowing it, lived under his dominion. But at the moment Jesus became my Lord, I was born again. At that moment, I received all that salvation held for me; life, the mind of Christ, healing for my body, deliverance from every evil, and abundant provision for life, and it was all eternal, everlasting. At that moment, I had no real idea of what I had received, but I did know that Jesus loved me and that I loved Him and wanted to serve Him. I had to learn over the intervening years of all that was provided to me in that experience. The experience of salvation is but the starting point of an eternal walk with Jesus. And it is in that walk that I have learned all I know of what I possess today, and have possessed since that experience.

I was lost, but now I'm found, forever. I was spiritually dead, but now I'm alive, forever. My mind was conformed to the world, but now it is transformed, and continually so, forever. I was a candidate for sickness and disease, but now I'm healed, forever. I was a candidate for bondage, but now I'm delivered, forever. I was designated to suffer a lifetime of poverty, lack, and shortage, but now I live with abundant provision, forever. The life I received through Jesus holds it all, and it is mine forever. My Father has given me all things that pertain to life and godliness through the knowledge of the Lord Jesus Christ, and it's mine forever.

In all we've examined so far, we have done so considering, or remembering, the body of Jesus that was broken for us for our healing. But there is much yet to consider. While we must never forget that it was by His stripes that we were healed (Isaiah 53:4-5; 1 Peter 2:24), we must also remember that by remembering the body of Jesus being broken, we are also reminded of the present condition of so much division that exists within the body of Christ. By remembering His body broken, we can realize that in that brokenness lies the revelation of how the body of Christ can function today as a body united.

Within the body of Christ in the earth today, there are surely billions of members, and most of us do not know one another. Yet being His body, we are all connected as the Church in the earth. In each member of His body in the earth you will find His spiritual DNA. Yet at the same moment, each member of His body is a peculiar treasure with its own unique function. For that to exist, Father has placed in each member of the body of Christ certain talents, anointings, and giftings that make each member a valuable and vital part of the body. The Scriptures tell us plainly that every member of the body of Christ is needful. In fact, the head of the body, which is Jesus, cannot say to the feet, the furthest removed part of the body from the head, "I have no need of thee" (1 Corinthians 12:12-27). Whoever you are, whatever your name, if Jesus is your Lord, you are needed in the body of Christ.

It is your uniqueness, your talents, anointings, and giftings, and your placement in the body that makes you valuable and vital to the body of Christ. Until you recognize that about yourself, you will always be battling your mind and the devices of Satan that work to give you a sense of unworthiness and uselessness to the body of Christ. As long as you entertain such thinking, your true worth to the body of Christ will be hidden from you and never enjoyed by the body, honor the Lord, or glorify your heavenly Father.

When you partake of the bread, the broken body of Jesus, clearly remember that He was broken for you **AND** anyone and everyone who has and yet will receive Him as Lord and Savior. For that reason, whenever you look upon another believer, do so with a conscious effort and faith in God to help you recognize the talents, anointings, and giftings set in them by the Holy Trinity, Father, Son, and Holy Ghost. Then, upon recognizing them, exercise your faith for Holy Ghost to help you demonstrate proper honor for that set of talents, anointings, and giftings so you can "provoke (one another) unto love and to good works" (Hebrews 10:24). In so doing, our remembrance of the broken body of Jesus brings glory to God, edification to the body, and blessing upon the body.

And one more thing needs to be added here. We are told in Ephesians 4 that the five-fold ministry (apostle, prophet, evangelist, pastor, and teacher) is given for the perfecting of the saints, for the work of the ministry, for the edifying of the body of Christ, until "we all come in the unity of the faith," and much more. Please take time to recognize and understand that remembering the broken body of Jesus and functioning in faith with that remembrance makes you a progenitor of unity within the body of Christ. It is this provocation to unity in the faith that moves us closer by each breath to the glorious body without spot, wrinkle, or blemish for which our Lord will return.

- The Cup -

But we need to look further into this fellowship with the Lord through Communion, and see what Jesus said to us about His blood that was shed for us for the remission of sins. It is the blood of Jesus that cleanses us from sin. Without the shedding of blood, there is no remission of sins (Hebrews 9:22). It is His blood, the blood of Jesus, that continually cleanses us from all sin **IF** we walk in the light as He is in the light (1 John 1:7).

Too often we fail to remember the wide-reaching eternal efficacy of the shed blood of Jesus Christ. Think of this. In the Old Covenant, when a man who was walking in covenant with the Lord died, he could not go to heaven. There was a special place reserved for those we call the Old Testament saints. It was called Paradise, or Upper Sheol, and also Abraham's bosom. You see, when Adam was first placed in the Garden of Eden, Father gave him dominion over all the handiworks of His hand, up to, but not including His throne. So, when Adam committed high treason against God, his sin tainted all that which had been placed under his authority. And once again, that reached all the way up to, but not including, Father's throne. That is why in the Old Testament, Satan had the right to come into the presence of Jehovah God as we see in the book of Job.

Because of Adam's sin, and its far-reaching consequences, even heaven was not a fit place for man to come in the Old Testament. Therefore, Father created that place we call Upper Sheol, Paradise, or Abraham's bosom, where those under his covenant could rest until things changed.

Now remember that after Jesus had shed His blood, and arose, when Mary reached out to touch Him, He told her not to touch Him, for He had not yet ascended to the Father God. Later the same day, He told his disciples to "handle me, for a spirit hath not flesh and bone as you see I have" (Luke 24:39). What took place between those two moments. Jesus had ascended to the Father, applied His blood to the heavenly vessels of worship, cleansed all of heaven, preached to the Old Testament saints in Upper Sheol, and led them out of that captivity so they could join Him when He ascended to the right hand of the Father. Oh, how I thank God for the cleansing power of the blood of Jesus!

It was that blood, the blood of Jesus Christ, God's first begotten Son, that was the cup of the covenant Jesus offered His disciples at the Last Supper. And once again I remind you that Jesus said we are to take that cup "in remembrance" of Him. And it is that same cup of which Paul writes when he said we are take that cup "in remembrance" of the Lord Jesus Christ. Let's remember.

The first and foremost element in remembering the cup of the Lord Jesus is that His blood was shed for the remission of sin. Without His blood, not a single human being could be redeemed, made righteous, and live in the newness of life that is in Christ Jesus. But the moment you acted upon Romans 10:9-10, confessing with your mouth the Lordship of Jesus Christ, believing in your heart that God had raised Him from the dead, you were saved. That salvation made you the immediate recipient of all salvation holds; the new birth, the availability of the renewed mind, a healed body, total deliverance from all evil, and abundant provision of every need you could ever experience in your life. It was the blood of Jesus that removed the sin nature from you at the moment of the new birth, washing and making you clean from all unrighteousness.

Now, as a Christian, should you sin, you have an Advocate with Father, the righteous Christ Jesus, Who is faithful and just to forgive you that sin and cleanse you afresh with His blood from all unrighteousness, restoring you to right fellowship with your heavenly Father. And that cleansing agent is the same blood that washed you from your sin nature when you were born again. The blood of Jesus never fails.

When the blood of Jesus cleanses you from sin, whatever that sin may have been, it restores you to that place in Christ where that sin is completely washed away, never to be remembered against you, never to be brought up about you again. My friend, that is a wonderful place to stand in Jesus, washed in His blood, free from sin, having been made the righteousness of God, and having the ability to live free of any sin consciousness, possessing only a righteousness consciousness (Hebrews 9-10).

That same blood continues its work today. According to 1 John 1:7, if you walk in the light as He is in the light, not only do you have fellowship with the Father, but His blood continually cleanses you from all sin. It is, as songwriters have penned, "a fountain filled with blood, drawn from Emmanuel's veins," and "Oh, the blood of Jesus that washes white as snow." Thank God for the blood of Jesus.

But as great as it is to be completely washed from all sin by the blood of Jesus, His blood does yet more. Leviticus 17:11 declares, “the life of the flesh is in the blood.” Consider those words. Are you a Christian? If so, you have been washed in the blood. You are a member of the body of Christ of which Jesus is the Head. The same life that is in the Head is in the body; in you; in every cell of your being.

When you were born again, the blood of Jesus, having cleansed you from all sin, began to live in you. Paul declared, “I am crucified with Christ: nevertheless I live; yet not I, but Christ liveth in me: and the life which I now live in the flesh I live by the faith of the Son of God, who loved me, and gave himself for me.” When we accept this great truth in the light that the life of the flesh in the blood, the connection becomes absolute. The life that you receive when you’re born again is the very life of Christ. It is **ETERNAL, EVERLASTING** life. And that life exists in you by the blood of Jesus. His blood becomes your life, for it is His blood, and His blood alone that carries **ETERNAL, EVERLASTING** life.

Oh, how every believer should rejoice in the life they have flowing through the very veins of their body! My spirit man thrills when I say the words that the life I now live is not my life, but the life of Christ, Who gave Himself for me so I can live in Him. What a joy should be the manifest possession of every believer because he has been made clean by the blood, and being made clean, also has the very life of God flowing in his veins. What a wonderful and marvelous double blessing that is ours through the blood of Jesus!

Ah, but there is yet more. However, before I continue to write about this, I urge you to take the time to read Genesis 4:1-17, and Hebrews 11 and 12. In Genesis we read that Abel's blood cried out to God from the ground. Cain had killed his brother, and though dead, Abel's blood yet cried out unto God. We read of that again in Hebrews 11, and in chapter 12 we read of the blood of Jesus, the "blood of sprinkling" that yet speaks. It is said of the "blood of sprinkling" that it "speaks better things *than that* of Abel."

Because Abel's blood cried out to God from the ground, Cain was cursed from the earth. But because the blood of Jesus cries out, Jesus being our Intercessor, our Mediator between God and man, we are not cursed, but blessed. And that blessing is ours from all of God's creation. Think of it. In the beginning, God created all that was created to serve His man, and then He gave dominion over all creation to the man it was to serve. Adam lost it to Satan in the fall, but Jesus has redeemed it back. Now, the earth is the Lord's, and the fullness thereof; the world, and all they that dwell therein" (Psalm 24:1). Satan may be the god of this world, but he does not own it. Jesus took it back, and having done that, returned it into the hands of His people, the Church of the Lord Jesus Christ. Now we are to go in His Name. Whatever we ask the Father in His Name He will give us. If we ask anything in His Name, He will do it.

My friend, that is fixed forever. That is His Word. Immutable, unchanging, settled forever in heaven, and upholding all things by its power. Oh, how the old hymn of the church rings in my heart. "There is power, power, wonder working power in the blood of the Lamb." It is our cleansing, our life, our victory, and an interceding voice unto God; the "precious blood of the Lamb."

Allow me to exhort you right now. As soon as you are in a place where you can do so, stop, and set aside before yourself the elements of Communion; the bread and the cup. Follow the commands of the Lord Jesus and receive both the bread and the cup "**in remembrance**" of all the Lord has provided for you in this observation. You don't need to be in a church service, or at the church. You don't need your pastor present. You have just received a clear and accurate statement of the work, purpose, and function of Communion. Take your time in your own personal observation of this ordinance.

Remember His body broken for you. Yes, you personally. It was broken for your healing. You received your healing when you were born again. Remember that. Having received your healing, you are now, already healed. Remember that. You no longer have to ask to receive that which has already been given, but you will surely have to fight the good fight of faith to keep what you have received through Christ's broken body.

Remember His blood shed for you. Yes, you personally. His blood has cleansed you from sin. If you are aware of sin in your life, confess it immediately, put your full faith and confidence in His Word and His blood. The blood still cleanses from all unrighteousness. Remember that. Remember that the life in your body is His life, for it is His blood that has cleansed you, and now flows through you. You have divine life flowing in, to, and through every cell of your being. And remember that the blood that was shed by Jesus, that same blood that is flowing through you at this moment, yet speaks of better things. Put your full faith and confidence in the Word that the blood of Jesus that cleanses you, the blood of Jesus that courses divine life through your being, the blood of Jesus that still speaks of better things, speaks for you to Father, with you in Jesus, and to you by Holy Spirit.

I bless you in the Name of Jesus as you partake of the body and the blood of Jesus. May you ever be thrilled as never before when you come to the Lord's table to receive of "the bread" and "the cup."

Conclusion

So, what can we say in summation? I believe four words will suffice. They are simple words that are obviously connected to the title of this book. Here are the words.

It's all about covenant!

Over the years one can choose phrases that stick with them. One such phrase that has been a part of my regular vocabulary now for more than two decades is "If God said it, that settles it." I remember that for years I would see bumper stickers on cars that read, "God said it, I believe, and that settles it." One day I saw that bumper sticker and it really aggravated me. I suddenly saw the gross error in its verbiage. You see, if God said, that settles it, whether you believe it or not.

So, there you have it. I have written to you about our Covenant of Health provided to us by our Lord. I believe that what I have written is accurate and soundly based on the Word of God; on covenant. Our covenant is what God has said to us in His Word. And in that covenant, we have clear and defining statements showing the demonstration of God's ability and the declaration of His will. It can all be concluded in these words . . .

If God said it, that settles it.

God's blessing be upon you through His Covenant.

About the Author

Beechard Moorefield was born April 29, 1949. At this publishing, he has lived during the administration of fourteen presidents. He holds an Associate Degree in Police Science, a Bachelor's Degree in Commercial Music, a Master's Degree in Organizational Management, an MBA, and a Doctor of Divinity. He has been engaged in pulpit ministry since 1971, serving as the Pastor of New Life International Pentecostal Fellowship for 28 of those years.

His wife of 50 years, Sharon, is his partner and key encourager in all he does. They have two sons, Alex and Jason, both professional men, and two grandsons. His interests in life have been many and varied. He is an accomplished musician (guitarist) and vocalist. He has been involved in martial arts for more than 50 years, holding second degree Black Belts in two different styles. He now enjoys shooting, traveling, and learning, especially helping people, and having time with his family.

He is a certified leadership coach, teacher, trainer, and speaker with the John Maxwell Group, and leads his own leadership training organization, Eagles Nest Forum, with offices in his hometown of Winston-Salem, North Carolina. His entire life, all he does, and his international work in training Christian leaders is Biblically based, and Christ-centered. He lives to lift people higher.

Purchase Information

Information pertaining to
Covenant of Health – Beyond a Promise,
may be obtained by contacting the author
through the office of
Eagles Nest Forum, Incorporated.

Eagles Nest Publishing Books
may be ordered by contacting:

Eagles Nest Publishing
A Division of Eagles Nest Forum, Inc.
www.eaglesnestforum.com
moorefieldbeechard@gmail.com
1.336.399.4288
1.336.659.0863

The price is $15.00 per copy, and shipping and handling will be an additional $5.00.

The cost for more than ten copies, including shipping, will be negotiable.